WORKPLACE LEARNING & PERFORMANCE ROLES

The ANALYST

WILLIAM J. ROTHWELL

A Self-Guided Job Aid With Assessments Based on
ASTD Models for Workplace Learning and Performance

CD-ROM
INCLUDED

*Linking People,
Learning & Performance*

Ordering information: Books published by the American Society for Training & Development can be ordered by calling 800.628.2783 or 703.683.8100, or via the Website at www.astd.org.

Library of Congress Catalog Card Number: 00-100862

ISBN: 1-56286-138-7

◢ TABLE OF CONTENTS

                                                                                    Page

List of Tables and Figures iv

Section 1   **Getting Started** 1
              ♦ What Is the Background of This Project? 3
              ♦ What Does This Job Aid Contain, and How Do You Use It? 3

Section 2   **Defining the Role of Analyst** 5
              ♦ Definitions 7
              ♦ Importance of the Analyst's Role 7
              ♦ The Relationship Between the Analyst's Role and the Evaluator's Role 7
              ♦ What Are Competencies, and Why Are They Important? 8
              ♦ Competencies Associated With the Role of Analyst 8
              ♦ Difference Between a Performance Problem and a Performance Improvement
                Opportunity 10
              ♦ The Place of Analysis in the Human Performance Improvement Process 10
              ♦ Outputs Associated With the Role of Analyst 11
              ♦ Who Performs the Role of Analyst? 11
              ♦ When Do They Perform This Role? 16
              ♦ What Is the Scope of the Projects That Analysts Carry Out? 17

Section 3   **Enacting the Role of Analyst** 19
              ♦ A Model of the Analysis Process 21
              ♦ *Step 1*: Determine the Current Performance Environment 24
              ♦ *Step 2*: Document the Results Obtained 27
              ♦ *Step 3*: Establish the Desired Results 34
              ♦ *Step 4*: Create a System for Measuring What Is to Be Measured 36
              ♦ *Step 5*: Determine the Current Level of Awareness 41
              ♦ *Step 6*: Determine the Current Level of Commitment 43
              ♦ *Step 7*: Assess the Future Environment 50
              ♦ *Step 8*: Uncover the Reasons for Performance Gaps .55

Section 4   **Tools for Conducting Analysis** 59
              ♦ Introduction to the Tools Section 61

Section 5   **Afterword** 83
              ♦ Why Is It Important to Master the Role of Analyst and the Competencies
                Associated With It? 85
              ♦ How Does It Feel to Perform the Role of Analyst? 85
              ♦ What Should You Do Next? 85

Bibliography 87

About the Author 91

LIST OF TABLES AND FIGURES

Section 2   **Table 2.1:** Competencies Associated With the Analyst's Role .9

Table 2.2: Sample Outputs Associated With the Analyst's Role 11

Figure 2.1: The Human Performance Improvement Process Model 11

Figure 2.2: Worksheet to Organize Your Thinking on Your Organization's Work Expectations for the Analyst's Role 12

Section 3   **Table 3.1:** Relationship Between Analysis and the Competencies of the Analyst 22

Figure 3.1: Model of Analysis 21

Figure 3.2: Step 1: Determine the Current Performance Environment 25

Figure 3.3: The Performance Environment 26

Figure 3.4: Instrument for Assessing Employee Opinions About Performance Conditions 28

Figure 3.5: Step 2: Document the Results Obtained 30

Figure 3.6: The DACUM Process: A Powerful Tool for Achieving Improved Performance 31

Figure 3.7: Step 3: Establish the Desired Results 34

Figure 3.8: Step 4: Create a System for Measuring What Is to Be Measured 37

Figure 3.9: Sources of Information About Hard Performance Gaps 38

Figure 3.10: Sources of Information About Soft Performance Gaps 38

Figure 3.11: Worksheet for Conducting Goal Analysis 40

Figure 3.12: Step 5: Determine the Current Level of Awareness 42

Figure 3.13: Grid to Assess Awareness 43

Figure 3.14: Step 6: Determine the Current Level of Commitment 44

Figure 3.15: Worksheet for Organizing a Proposal 46

Figure 3.16: Instrument for Measuring Awareness of a Performance Problem 47

Figure 3.17: Instrument for Measuring Commitment to Solving a Performance Problem 48

Figure 3.18: Score Evaluations for Awareness and Commitment Instruments 49

Figure 3.19: Step 7: Assess the Future Environment 50

Figure 3.20: Environmental Monitoring for Workplace Learning and Performance 51

Figure 3.21: Environmental Scanning as Part of the Analysis Process 52

Figure 3.22: Environmental Sectors 53

Figure 3.23: Step 8: Uncover the Reasons for Performance Gaps 55

Section 4   **Figure 4.1:** Worksheet to Guide Comprehensive Analysis 62

Figure 4.2: Root Cause Analysis 78

Figure 4.3: Cause-and-Effect Diagram 80

Figure 4.4: Process Charting 82

SECTION 1	GETTING STARTED

- ◆ What Is the Background of This Project?
- ◆ What Does This Job Aid Contain, and How Do You Use It?

SECTION 2	DEFINING THE ROLE OF ANALYST

SECTION 3	ENACTING THE ROLE OF ANALYST

SECTION 4	TOOLS FOR CONDUCTING ANALYSIS

SECTION 5	AFTERWORD

SECTION 1   GETTING STARTED

What Is the Background of This Project?

The Analyst is an outgrowth of *ASTD Models for Workplace Learning and Performance* (Rothwell, Sanders, and Soper, 1999). It is a self-study job aid for the workplace learning and performance (WLP) practitioner that describes the competencies essential for success in the WLP field and contains information about the practitioner's role as analyst. (Additional volumes in this ASTD series will focus on the practitioner's other roles. See ASTD's Website, www.astd.org, for information on these volumes as they are released.) Note that the term *role* here should not be confused with job title; rather, just as in theater the word *role* refers to the part that an actor plays, in WLP a role is a part that the practitioner plays in the human performance improvement (HPI) process. Following is a complete list of WLP roles (see also Rothwell et al., 1999, pages xv-xvii):

♦ The *manager* plans, organizes, schedules, and leads the work of individuals and groups to achieve desired results; facilitates the strategic plan; ensures that workplace learning and performance accord with organizational needs and plans; and ensures accomplishment of the administrative requirements of the function.

♦ The *analyst* isolates and troubleshoots the causes of "human performance gaps" and identifies areas in need of improvement.

♦ The *intervention selector* chooses appropriate learning and performance *interventions* (that is, corrective actions), both in and out of the workplace, to address the causes of these performance gaps.

♦ The *intervention designer and developer* formulates learning and performance interventions that

address these causes and complement similarly targeted interventions.

♦ The *intervention implementor* ensures that the interventions that have been selected are carried out in an effective and appropriate way and complements similarly targeted interventions. In this capacity, the intervention implementor may serve as, for example, administrator, instructor, organization development practitioner, career development specialist, process redesign consultant, workspace designer, compensation specialist, or facilitator.

♦ The *change leader* inspires the workforce to embrace the interventions implemented, creates a direction for the effort, and ensures that the interventions are continually monitored and directed in ways that are consistent with stakeholders' desired results.

♦ The *evaluator* assesses the changes made, the actions taken, the results achieved, and the impact experienced and apprises participants and stakeholders accordingly.

What Does This Job Aid Contain, and How Do You Use It?

The Analyst consists of both a book and an accompanying CD-ROM that is designed to enhance and test your knowledge. Read the written material first, then use the CD-ROM to assess what you have learned. Practice using the worksheets and activities. For additional input, be sure to ask mentors or knowledgeable co-workers for one-on-one coaching.

| **SECTION 1** | GETTING STARTED |

| **SECTION 2** | DEFINING THE ROLE OF ANALYST |

◆ Definitions

◆ Importance of the Analyst's Role

◆ The Relationship Between the Analyst's Role and the Evaluator's Role

◆ What Are Competencies, and Why Are They Important?

◆ Competencies Associated With the Role of Analyst

◆ Difference Between a Performance Problem and a Performance Improvement Opportunity

◆ The Place of Analysis in the Human Performance Improvement Process

◆ Outputs Associated With the Role of Analyst

◆ Who Performs the Role of Analyst?

◆ When Do They Perform This Role?

◆ What Is the Scope of the Projects That Analysts Carry Out?

| **SECTION 3** | ENACTING THE ROLE OF ANALYST |

| **SECTION 4** | TOOLS FOR CONDUCTING ANALYSIS |

| **SECTION 5** | AFTERWORD |

Definitions

As we noted in the preceding section, the WLP practitioner's role as analyst is to isolate and troubleshoot the causes of human performance gaps and identify areas for improvement. In other words, it is the analyst's task to identify (or help others to identify) disparities between actual performance and desired performance—and, where such disparities exist, to determine the reasons that underlie them. (The term *performance* here refers to the positive outcomes of work.)

The analyst's role consists of, but is not limited to, organizational analysis (sometimes called organizational diagnosis), operations analysis (sometimes called process improvement), individual analysis, performance analysis (sometimes called front-end analysis), and training needs assessment (TNA). We define these terms in the following paragraph.

Organizational analysis is a systematic examination of an organization's strengths and weaknesses. *Operations analysis* is an examination of how the organization's work is organized or performed. *Individual analysis* is an assessment of the people who perform the work, their capacities to learn, and their "fit" with the work to which they are assigned. *Performance analysis* is "an attempt at a method of disciplining ourselves as we seek to delineate our problems before we rush into a solution" (Gilbert, 1982, page 22). *Training needs assessment* is "the systematic study of a problem or innovation, incorporating data and opinions from varied sources, in order to make effective decisions or recommendations about what should happen next" (Rossett, 1987, page 3).

As important as TNA is, the analyst's role is by no means confined to it. Analysts must take into account the organizational context in which performance is to be achieved, the work processes by which that performance is carried out, and the match between the people who do the work and what they have to think, do, or feel in order to achieve the desired results. In addition, analysts "identify gaps in results, place them in order of priority, and select the most important for closure or reduction" (Watkins and Kaufman, 1996, page 13). Finally, they "identify the causes of the gaps in results so that appropriate methods, means, tactics, tools, and approaches may be identified rationally and then selected for meeting the needs" (Watkins and Kaufman, 1996, page 13).

Importance of the Analyst's Role

No human performance problem can be solved until the facts and perceptions surrounding it are understood, and it is the analyst's role to clarify those facts and perceptions. Moreover, while analysis is a fundamental first step in any WLP effort, it is also "considered the most critical," as Richard Swanson notes in *Analysis for Improving Performance: Tools for Diagnosing Organizations and Documenting Workplace Expertise* (1994, page 8), since it "defines, frames, and directs the remaining steps."

Without the analyst, for example, the intervention selector would not be able to make appropriate choices: He or she would be unsure of what is causing a problem, what facts or issues surround it, who is interested in making improvements to it, what business needs are intended to be met by those improvements, and what results are desired. Lacking information from the analyst, the intervention selector would likely treat symptoms rather than underlying causes. Likewise, just as it is the analyst's role to uncover facts and perceptions surrounding performance problems and isolate their cause(s), it is the evaluator's role to verify those facts and perceptions.

The Relationship Between the Analyst's Role and the Evaluator's Role

The roles of analyst and evaluator are closely related and can be easily confused. For this reason, it is important to distinguish between them. While analysts identify performance problems and determine their causes, evaluators assess the results or impacts of interventions. In other words, analysts uncover *problems* and isolate their cause(s), while evaluators examine the *solutions* (interventions) and determine their results. Analysts and evaluators may pose similar questions, though their intentions may differ. Analysts want to find out what problems exist and what causes them. Evaluators want to find out whether interventions solved the problems, addressed the causes, and provided value-added benefits to the organization and its people.

Of course, there are occasions when the work of analyst and evaluator can be performed closely together. Although analysts typically perform their work before an intervention, these role distinctions can blur because evaluators can perform their work before, during, and after interventions. That can create some confusion—especially before an intervention when an analyst is interested in determining the cause of a problem while an evaluator might be interested in forecasting the benefits of a solution. Furthermore, it is possible that the same person may (or may not) be enacting both roles.

Both analysts and evaluators also share several competencies. For instance, both must apply the competency analytical thinking. But analysts apply that competency to problems and their consequences (effects), while evaluators apply it to solutions and their outcomes. Both analysts and evaluators also must apply the competency performance gap analysis, which compares actual and ideal performance levels. Here, analysts focus their attention on the differences before an intervention is undertaken, while evaluators may focus their attention on the differences before, during, and after the intervention is undertaken. If analysts have enacted their role successfully, evaluators should not need to repeat the work performed by them. (If that is not the case or if different people enact these roles, double-checking may be necessary.)

Unique to the evaluator's role are such competencies as analyzing performance data and intervention monitoring. By definition, analyzing performance data occurs after an intervention is undertaken and is intended to determine the intervention's effects. Intervention monitoring focuses attention on aligning the intervention with organizational strategies during implementation.

What Are Competencies, and Why Are They Important?

Competencies are characteristics that underlie successful performance: "internal capabilities that people bring to their jobs, capabilities which may be expressed in a broad, even infinite, array of on-the-job behaviors" (McLagan, 1989, page 77). Competencies have commanded growing attention because they distinguish the *exemplary* performers (best-in-class) from the *fully successful* (standard, but nothing more) performers. In other words, competencies are any knowledge, skill, attitude, motivation, or personal characteristic that leads to successful performance.

A *competency model* is a narrative description of the requirements for success in a job, department, or organization—a description of what should be. As such, it provides a standard against which individuals or groups can be assessed for development, as well as a foundation for (among other things) multi-rater, full-circle assessment; individual development planning; and career counseling. By building competencies, individuals, including WLP practitioners, can position themselves for career success (Rothwell and Lindholm, 1999).

Competencies Associated With the Role of Analyst

Descriptions of the competencies associated with the analyst's role can be found in Rothwell, Sanders, and Soper (1999) and are shown in table 2.1.

These competencies represent a set of skills that help the analyst bring clarity to problems ranging from the operational to the strategic. In other words, the analyst should first of all be able to compare actual performance to the ideal and recognize how to address any problems with the gap or difference. This is called *performance gap analysis*.

Next, the analyst should be able to break down complicated issues (*analytical thinking*), examine the characteristics that individuals and groups need to perform their work optimally (*competency identification*), and build models or descriptions of actual and desired work processes and activities (*model building*).

Third, the analyst should assess the likely impact of implementing solutions (*performance theory*) against the backdrop of the organization's political and other realities (*social awareness*).

Fourth, the analyst should be capable of making clear the results that are desired (*standards identification*), recognizing the interrelationships among issues (*systems thinking*), and understanding how performance issues are affected by the work environment (*work environment analysis; ability to see the "big picture"; business knowledge; identification of critical business issues; industry awareness; quality implications*).

Fifth, the analyst should be able to communicate to others both the problems and the interventions undertaken to address them (*communication; communication networks*), manage the stress (both in

Table 2.1: Competencies Associated with the Analyst's Role

Competencies Unique to the Analyst

- *Business knowledge:* Awareness of business functions and how business decisions affect financial and nonfinancial work results
- *Competency identification:* Defining the skills, knowledge, and attitudes required to perform the work
- *Coping skills:* Dealing with ambiguity and stress resulting from conflicting information and goals; helping others deal with ambiguity and stress
- *Ethics modeling:* Defining exemplary ethical behavior and understanding the implications
- *Group dynamics:* Assessing how groups of people function and evolve as they seek to meet the needs of their members and of the organization
- *Identification of critical business issues:* Determining key business issues and forces for change and applying that knowledge to performance improvement strategies
- *Industry awareness:* Understanding the current and future climate of the organization's industry and formulating strategies that respond to that climate
- *Model building:* Conceptualizing and developing theoretical and practical frameworks that describe complex ideas
- *Social awareness:* Seeing organizations as dynamic political, economic, and social systems
- *Survey design and development:* Creating survey approaches that use open-ended (essay) and closed (multiple choice and Likert) questions for collecting data; preparing instruments in written, verbal, or electronic formats

Competencies Shared By Both the Analyst and the Evaluator

- *Ability to see the "big picture":* Identifying trends and patterns that are outside the normal paradigm of the organization
- *Analytical thinking:* Breaking down complex issues into meaningful components and synthesizing related items
- *Communication:* Applying effective verbal, nonverbal, and written communication methods to achieve desired results
- *Communication networks:* Understanding the various methods through which communication is achieved
- *Interpersonal relationship building:* Interacting effectively with others in order to produce meaningful outcomes
- *Performance gap analysis:* Performing a front-end analysis by comparing actual and ideal performance levels in the workplace and identifying opportunities and strategies for performance improvement
- *Performance theory:* Recognizing the implications, outcomes, and consequences of performance interventions to distinguish between activities and results
- *Quality implications:* Identifying interrelationships and implications among quality programs and performance
- *Questioning:* Collecting data via pertinent questions in surveys, interviews, and focus groups for the purpose of performance analysis
- *Standards identification:* Determining what constitutes success for individuals, organizations, and processes

(continued on next page)

Competencies Shared By Both the Analyst and the Evaluator *(continued)*

◆ *Systems thinking:* Recognizing interrelationships among events by determining the driving forces that connect seemingly isolated incidents within the organization; taking a holistic view of performance problems in order to find causes

◆ *Technlogical literacy:* Understanding and appropriately applying existing, new, or emerging technologies

◆ *Work environment analysis:* Examining the work environment for issues or characteristics that affect human performance; understanding characteristics of a high-performance workplace

Source: Rothwell, W., Sanders, E., and Soper, J. (1999). *ASTD Models for Workplace Learning and Performance: Roles, Competencies, and Outputs.* Alexandria, VA: ASTD.

themselves and in others) that accompanies analysis as a result of the anxiety produced by possible criticism of one's work *(coping skills)*, work effectively with others *(interpersonal relationship building; group dynamics)*, and demonstrate an ethical approach to their activities *(ethics modeling)*.

Sixth, the analyst should apply to his or her communications whatever variety of questioning techniques is necessary for eliciting information *(questioning; survey design and development)*.

Last, the analyst should understand the potential effects of technology on performance and interpersonal relationships in the organization *(technological literacy)*.

Among the competencies identified in Rothwell (1996a), research for a doctoral dissertation by Stephen King (1998) reported that in a questionnaire sent to 1,000 members of the International Society for Performance Improvement (response rate, 33.3 percent), practitioners named performance analysis *(front-end analysis)* to be the single most important skill necessary for success.

Difference Between a Performance Problem and a Performance Improvement Opportunity

A *human performance problem* is the difference between actual results and desired or optimal results. *Actual results* mean current conditions. *Desired results* reflect what decision makers and other stakeholders

say they want. *Optimal results* are the best results possible.

The world is filled with human performance problems—for example, situations in which production, customer service, or product quality fall below expectations. In each such situation, corrective action (in the field called an *intervention*) needs to be taken.

A *human performance improvement opportunity* represents a possibility for enhancing production, quality, or service when no problems otherwise appear to exist; it is a fine-tuning of an already well-functioning system. It is, for example, an entrepreneur's ability to spot otherwise unnoticed ways of meeting a need, creating a demand, or reducing the number of steps necessary for a production process. Such opportunities range from a small-scale change to a large-scale change.

Throughout this book the term *performance problem* will be used to mean both the difference between actual and desired results and performance improvement opportunities.

The Place of Analysis in the Human Performance Improvement Process

Analysis occurs early in the HPI process, the guiding model for WLP (see figure 2.1), and comprises both performance analysis and cause analysis. *Performance analysis* is the process of identifying the organization's performance requirements and comparing them to

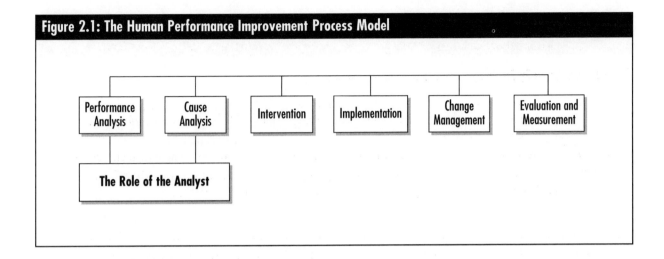

Figure 2.1: The Human Performance Improvement Process Model

```
        ┌──────────┬──────────┬──────────┬──────────┬──────────┐
  ┌──────────┐ ┌──────────┐ ┌──────────┐ ┌──────────────┐ ┌──────────┐ ┌──────────────┐
  │Performance│ │   Cause  │ │Intervention│ │Implementation│ │  Change  │ │Evaluation and│
  │  Analysis │ │  Analysis │ │           │ │              │ │Management│ │ Measurement  │
  └──────────┘ └──────────┘ └──────────┘ └──────────────┘ └──────────┘ └──────────────┘
        │
  ┌──────────────────────┐
  │ The Role of the Analyst │
  └──────────────────────┘
```

its objectives and capabilities. Following performance analysis is *cause analysis*—the process, with the object of improving productivity or competitiveness, of determining the reasons for past and present performance gaps and the potential for any such gaps in the future.

Outputs Associated With the Role of Analyst

Output is the term used to refer to the results of analytic processes. (For sample outputs of analysis, see table 2.2.) However, the particular work outputs necessary in the analyst's role depend upon the unique requirements of an organization's corporate culture and work expectations. Take a moment to think about the corporate culture and work expec-

tations of your own organization by completing the worksheet in figure 2.2.

Who Performs the Role of Analyst?

The role of analyst may be played by WLP practitioners serving as external or internal consultants, line managers, employees, or any or all of the above. Each choice of who will conduct analysis has advantages and disadvantages.

The advantages of using external consultants include the fact that they often have expertise (and thus credibility) in the subject in question and experience in solving the given problem. Evidence of expertise like an academic degree, a successful track record in a comparable organization, or publications

Table 2.2: Sample Outputs Associated with the Analyst's Role

♦ Analytical methods that uncover the reasons for performance gaps
♦ Results of assessment
♦ Reports to key stakeholders of individual, group, or organizational change efforts about direction of such efforts
♦ Reports to executives that highlight the relationship between human performance and financial performance

Source: Rothwell, W., Sanders, E., and Soper, J. (1999). *ASTD Models for Workplace Learning and Performance: Roles, Competencies, and Outputs*. Alexandria, VA: ASTD.

Figure 2.2: Worksheet to Organize Your Thinking on Your Organization's Work Expectations for the Analyst's Role

Directions: Use this worksheet to organize your thinking about the work expectations that your organization has of you in the role of analyst. Remember that the analyst "troubleshoots to isolate the causes of human performance gaps or identifies areas for improving human performance." However, the outputs and quality requirements for the role of analyst may vary from one corporate culture to another. For each competency listed under column 1 below, describe under column 2 what you believe are the expectations for results—the outputs—in your organization. (You may need to discuss this issue with the organization's key decision makers and stakeholders.) Then, under column 3, describe what behaviors and quality requirements would demonstrate success with that competency. What results would you have to achieve to be considered successful by your customers and/or stakeholders? While there are no "right" or "wrong" answers, these questions are important for building the appropriate expectations among your customers and stakeholders. Take the time to discuss these issues.

	Column 1 Competency	Column 2 What do you believe are the organization's expectations for results (outputs) for the role of analyst?	Column 3 What behavior and/or quality requirements would demonstrate success with this competency in this organization? What results would you have to achieve to be considered successful by your customers and/or stakeholders?
1	*Ability to see the "big picture":* Identifying trends and patterns that are outside the normal paradigm of the organization		
2	*Analytical thinking:* Breaking down complex issues into meaningful components and synthesizing related items		
3	*Business knowledge:* Awareness of business functions and how business decisions affect financial and nonfinancial work results		
4	*Communication:* Applying effective verbal, nonverbal, and written communication methods to achieve desired results		

5	*Communication networks:* Understanding the various methods through which communication is achieved		
6	*Competency identification:* Defining the skills, knowledge, and attitudes required to perform the work		
7	*Coping skills:* Dealing with ambiguity and stress resulting from conflicting information and goals; helping others deal with ambiguity and stress		
8	*Ethics modeling:* Defining exemplary ethical behavior and understanding its implications		
9	*Group dynamics:* Assessing how groups of people function and evolve as they seek to meet the needs of their members and of the organization		
10	*Identification of critical business issues:* Determining key business issues and forces for change and applying that knowledge to performance improvement strategies		
11	*Industry awareness:* Understanding of the current and future climate of the organization's industry and formulating strategies that respond to that climate		
12	*Interpersonal relationship building:* Interacting effectively with others in order to produce meaningful outcomes		

(continued on next page)

Figure 2.2: Worksheet to Organize Your Thinking on Your Organization's Work Expectations for the Analyst's Role *(continued)*

	Column 1 Competency	Column 2 What do you believe are the organization's expectations for results (outputs) for the role of analyst?	Column 3 What behavior and/or quality requirements would demonstrate success with this competency in this organization? What results would you have to achieve to be considered successful by your customers and/or stakeholders?
13	*Model building:* Conceptualizing and developing theoretical and practical frameworks that communicate complex ideas		
14	*Performance gap analysis:* Performing front-end analysis by comparing actual and ideal performance levels in the workplace and identifying opportunities and strategies for performance improvement		
15	*Performance theory:* Recognizing the implications, outcomes, and consequences of performance interventions to distinguish between activities and results		
16	*Quality implications:* Identifying interrelationships and implications among quality programs and performance		
17	*Questioning:* Collecting data by means of pertinent questions in surveys, interviews, and focus groups for the purpose of performance analysis		

18	*Social awareness:* Seeing organizations as dynamic political, economic, and social systems		
19	*Standards identification:* Determining what constitutes success for individuals, organizations, and processes		
20	*Survey design and development:* Creating survey approaches that use open-ended (essay) and closed (multiple choice and Likert) questions for collecting data; preparing instruments in written, verbal, or electronic formats		
21	*Systems thinking:* Recognizing interrelationships among events by determining the driving forces that connect seemingly isolated incidents within the organization; taking a holistic view of performance problems in order to find causes		
22	*Technlogical literacy:* Understanding and appropriately applying existing, new, or emerging technologies		
23	*Work environment analysis:* Examining the work environment for issues or characteristics that affect human performance; understanding characteristics of a high-performance workplace		

on the subject may make it easier for external consultants to gain access to key stakeholders (for example, through meetings, phone calls, emails, and other methods), as well as license to recommend approaches that might not otherwise be acceptable in the corporate culture.

External consultants have the obvious disadvantage, however, that they are not as familiar as internal consultants, line managers, or employees with an organization's corporate culture, power structure, or work processes, or with the personalities and value systems of the organization's key decision makers. External consultants must find ways to familiarize themselves with such matters quickly and effectively.

Using internal consultants also has its advantages. For one thing, ordinarily, internal consultants are more familiar with the particular industry or business, to say nothing of an organization's particular corporate culture and informal processes. In addition, since internal consultants, as members of the organization, are not distracted by the demands of multiple clients, they are often in a better position than their counterparts from outside to facilitate long-term projects and day-to-day implementation.

The downside of using internal consultants is that they may lack the access to key decision makers that is often afforded external consultants, and they may not enjoy the same level of credibility; as the saying goes, no one is a prophet in his or her own homeland. In addition, the internal consultant may also lack objectivity regarding both personnel and processes.

Generally speaking, line managers and employees are most familiar with performance problems. But that familiarity can be both an advantage and a disadvantage. While obviously the people who are most intimately involved in a project know most about its details, such people may not necessarily have the competencies needed to function as an analyst. The good news is that line managers and employees can be trained in the competencies of the analyst's role.

Often the most powerful approach to analysis is to assemble a team of analysts from several sectors, whether external consultants working in tandem with internal ones, external consultants working with line managers and employees, or internal consultants working with line managers and employees.

When Do They Perform This Role?

The analyst's role is either requested by others or initiated by analysts themselves and is usually *situational*—in other words, it is called up in response to a particular performance problem at a particular time. Too often, in fact, crisis is the driver, and the analyst's role emerges only during the quest for solution.

When Requested by Others. Often WLP practitioners are approached to offer training—especially when either their job title or the name of the department to which they are attached leads others to believe that offering training is their chief responsibility. However, training is only one of many possible performance improvement strategies.

Unfortunately, not all problems are so simple that they can be solved by training alone—or, for that matter, by training at all. Clearly, when personnel lack the knowledge or skills they need to perform well, training is appropriate. But problems that have other causes call for other solutions.

Often formal training is the performance improvement strategy of last, rather than first, resort. The reason is that rigorous, results-oriented training is expensive, time-consuming, and difficult to design, field-test, deliver, and evaluate. Moreover, without management support and without planning to ensure that training transfers from off-site training to on-the-job practice, training alone cannot ensure individual or organizational change.

When approached for training, WLP practitioners in effect immediately take on the role of analyst, since prior to taking any other actions they should gather sufficient information about the situation, issue, or problem to determine whether training will be either all or part of a solution.

Consider the following vignettes and decide for yourself whether in each case training is called for.

Vignette 1: A line manager walks into the office of the company training director.

"My employees need customer service training," the manager says.

"Really?" responds the training director. "We have been offering customer service training for some time, and your employees have attended. Hasn't the training been effective?"

Vignette 2: "When we hire new employees," the company's vice president for human resources says to the training director, "they often lack many basic skills. We are going to have to start training people ourselves to communicate, handle stress, use computers, and make sound business decisions."

Vignette 3: "Even though most of our salespeople have more than 20 years' experience, they are not making enough sales," says the vice president for marketing. "Perhaps we should train them in the basic sales cycle."

In each of these situations, what questions would an analyst ask? How would an analyst handle each situation? What else might the analyst do?

When Initiated by the Analyst. Although often it is other people who prompt them to take on the role of analyst, WLP practitioners also have an obligation to be proactive—that is, to seek out performance problems. In such situations they are said to *initiate* the role of analyst.

WLP practitioners who enact the role of analyst face a greater challenge than do those who react to the requests of other people. As Niccolò Machiavelli wrote in *The Prince* (Random House, 1950, page 21), "There is nothing more difficult to carry out, nor more doubtful of success, nor more dangerous to handle, than to initiate a new order of things. For the reformer has enemies in all those who profit by the old order, and only lukewarm defenders in all those who might profit from the new."

In other words, WLP practitioners who initiate analysis do not have a ready constituency of supporters, the way they do when others have solicited their help. They must find and build support themselves.

In addition to seeking out the facts surrounding the problem they believe exists, they must find a sponsor or champion for the change—someone who can help build awareness of the problem and forge a commitment to action. And they may have to build a successful track record with their new approach or intervention, settling initially for small-scale pilot tests.

What Is the Scope of the Projects That Analysts Carry Out?

The term *project scope* refers to the size of the project that the analyst carries out, from small-scale to large. In addition, the project can be carried out as either a stand-alone effort or as an effort that is integrated with other projects.

The central question governing scope is, What is the size of the group experiencing the performance problem? Research suggests that as size increases, so does the complexity of the effort to institute change and the potential for conflict (Guy, 1986).

Typical small-scale projects include situations in which managers request training or another specific performance improvement intervention, such as an attitude survey, morale-building effort, or career fair. Such projects are often carried out as a single step in a multiple-step process. (For instance, in Instructional Systems Design, the decision to employ a training intervention is usually subsequent to an earlier performance analysis.)

Examples of large-scale efforts that call for the services of an analyst are situations in which the WLP practitioner is asked to help formulate a business strategy, create a team to generate organization-wide awareness of quality, spearhead a safety program, institute team-based management, or manage the implementation of a pay-for-knowledge program. In each of these cases, analysts may find themselves leading a long-term, fact-finding effort to scope out an intervention or to analyze perceptions. Large-scale projects are organized around an issue that needs to be addressed and may involve a team effort. One way to organize a large-scale project is to use the steps that characterize human performance analysis (see "Steps in Human Performance Analysis," 1996). When this approach is used, the analyst

♦ **aligns** (that is, makes sure that the client and the analysis team share an understanding of the project's focus, plan, and measures of success).

— Determines the client's business goals.

— Identifies the people who will directly affect the achievement of those goals.

— Identifies the work-process outputs produced by the people thus identified.

— Identifies deadlines and resource constraints that could affect the analysis project.

— Identifies data sources available to the analysis team.

— Establishes the project goal.

— Selects the appropriate type of analysis (new-performance or diagnostic).

♦ **analyzes** (that is, for new performance, conducts a human performance analysis to document new performance and identify human performance interventions required to support the desired performance).

— Verifies the process outputs produced by the target audience. Be sure to capture outputs that are out-of-the-ordinary.

— Collects data on the outputs, including time spent producing them.

— Produces a task list for each process output.

— Collects task data, including stimuli for initiating the task, speed requirements, and frequency of performance.

♦ **diagnoses** (that is, conducts a human performance analysis for whatever current performance fails to meet the organization's expectations; documents deficient performance; and identifies the human performance interventions required to achieve desired performance).

— Identifies and verifies deficient outputs that could impede the achievement of organizational goals.

— Produces task lists for each deficient output.

— Identifies which tasks are being performed inadequately. Determines the "who, what, when, and where" involved.

— Poses all feasible hypotheses for the causes of poor performance, including lack of skill or knowledge, poor motivation, and work environment barriers.

— Plans data collection; collects and analyzes evidence.

— Determines probable causes.

— Specifies appropriate interventions, such as training, job aids, job redesign, performance management, and electronic performance support systems (EPSSs).

♦ **plans** (that is, creates project plans for the design and implementation of appropriate interventions).

— Lists in order of priority the interventions to be designed and implemented.

— Develops specifications for the selection and assignment of employees.

— Develops specifications for such information support as training and documentation.

— Develops specifications for the redesign and enhancement of the work environment.

— Develops specifications for the redesign and enhancement of motivational factors.

— Develops a master plan.

SECTION 1 GETTING STARTED

SECTION 2 DEFINING THE ROLE OF ANALYST

SECTION 3 ENACTING THE ROLE OF ANALYST

- ◆ A Model of the Analysis Process
- ◆ *Step 1:* Determine the Current Performance Environment
- ◆ *Step 2:* Document the Results Obtained
- ◆ *Step 3:* Establish the Desired Results
- ◆ *Step 4:* Create a System for Measuring What Is to Be Measured
- ◆ *Step 5:* Determine the Current Level of Awareness
- ◆ *Step 6:* Determine the Current Level of Commitment
- ◆ *Step 7:* Assess the Future Environment
- ◆ *Step 8:* Uncover the Reasons for Performance Gaps

SECTION 4 TOOLS FOR CONDUCTING ANALYSIS

SECTION 5 AFTERWORD

◢ SECTION 3   ENACTING THE ROLE OF ANALYST

A *model* is a simplified depiction of a more complex object or process, and model building is an important part of analysis. A model of the analysis process can help WLP practitioners and others carry out analysis in a step-by-step fashion. Each step in the model is the basis for taking decisive action. Various models for analysis have been described (see Gilbert, 1978 and 1982; Mager and Pipe, 1984; Rothwell, 1996b; "Steps in Human Performance Analysis," 1996).

A Model of the Analysis Process

Think of the analysis process as a series of general steps as follows:

1. Determine the current performance environment.

2. Document the results obtained.

3. Establish the desired results.

4. Create a system for measuring what is to be measured.

5. Determine the current level of awareness.

6. Determine the current level of commitment.

7. Assess the future environment.

8. Uncover the reasons for performance gaps.

These steps are shown in figure 3.1, and their relationship to the analyst's competencies in table 3.1. This section addresses these steps and provides guidance for applying them. As you encounter performance problems, use figure 4.1, "A Worksheet to Guide Comprehensive Analysis," on page 62 to help pose questions related to each step of the model.

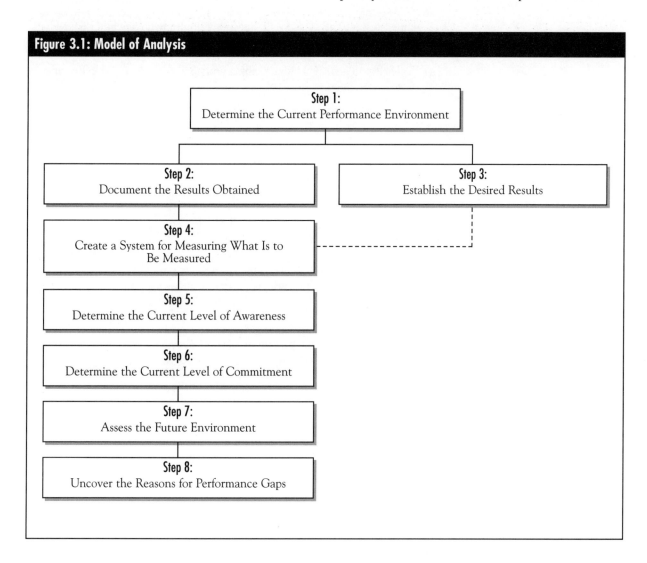

Figure 3.1: Model of Analysis

Step 1:
Determine the Current Performance Environment

Step 2:
Document the Results Obtained

Step 3:
Establish the Desired Results

Step 4:
Create a System for Measuring What Is to Be Measured

Step 5:
Determine the Current Level of Awareness

Step 6:
Determine the Current Level of Commitment

Step 7:
Assess the Future Environment

Step 8:
Uncover the Reasons for Performance Gaps

Table 3.1: Relationship Between Analysis and the Competencies of the Analyst*

Model of Analysis	Competencies of the Analyst
Determine the current performance environment	♦ *Ability to see the "big picture":* Identifying trends and patterns that are outside the normal paradigm of the organization ♦ *Identification of critical business issues:* Determining key business issues and forces for change and applying that knowledge to performance improvement strategies ♦ *Industry awareness:* Understanding the current and future climate of the organization's industry and formulating strategies that respond to that climate ♦ *Work environment analysis:* Examining the work environment for issues or characteristics that affect human performance; understanding characteristics of a high-performance workplace
Document the results obtained	♦ *Analytical thinking:* Clarifying complex issues by breaking them down into meaningful components and synthesizing related items ♦ *Questioning:* Collecting data via pertinent questions asked during surveys, interviews, and focus groups for the purpose of performance analysis ♦ *Survey design and development:* Creating survey approaches that use open-ended (essay) and closed style questions (multiple choice and Likert items) for collecting data; preparing instruments in written, verbal, or electronic formats ♦ *Technological literacy:* Understanding and appropriately applying existing, new, or emerging technology
Establish the desired results	♦ *Business knowledge:* Demonstrating awareness of business functions and how business decisions affect financial and nonfinancial work results ♦ *Competency identification:* Identifying the skills, knowledge, and attitudes required to perform work ♦ *Model building:* Conceptualizing and developing theoretical and practical frameworks that describe complex ideas ♦ *Quality implications:* Identifying the relationships and implications among quality programs and performance ♦ *Questioning:* Collecting data via pertinent questions asked during surveys, interviews, and focus groups for the purpose of performance analysis ♦ *Standards identification:* Determining what constitutes success for individuals, organizations, and processes ♦ *Survey design and development:* Creating survey approaches that use open-ended (essay) and closed style questions (multiple choice and Likert items) for collecting data; preparing instruments in written, verbal, or electronic formats ♦ *Technological literacy:* Understanding and appropriately applying existing, new, or emerging technology

*Some competencies are used in more than one step of the model.

Model of Analysis	Competencies of the Analyst
Create a system for measuring what is to be measured	♦ *Communication:* Applying effective verbal, nonverbal, and written communication methods to achieve desired results ♦ *Communicationn networks:* Understanding the various methods through which communication is achieved ♦ *Coping skills:* Dealing with ambiguity and stress resulting from conflicting information and goals; helping others deal with ambiguity and stress ♦ *Ethics modeling:* Modeling exemplary ethical behavior and understanding the implications of this responsibility ♦ *Group dynamics:* Assessing how groups of people function and evolve as they seek to meet the needs of their members and of the organization ♦ *Interpersonal relationship building:* Effectively interacting with others in order to produce meaningful outcomes ♦ *Performance gap analysis:* Performing front-end analysis by comparing actual and ideal performance levels in the workplace; identifying opportunities and strategies for performance improvement ♦ *Social awareness:* Seeing organizations as dynamic political, economic, and social systems
Determine the current level of awareness	♦ *Communication:* Applying effective verbal, nonverbal, and written communication methods to achieve desired results ♦ *Communication networks:* Understanding the various methods through which communication is achieved ♦ *Coping skills:* Dealing with ambiguity and stress resulting from conflicting information and goals; helping others deal with ambiguity and stress ♦ *Ethics modeling:* Modeling exemplary ethical behavior and understanding the implications of this responsibility ♦ *Group dynamics:* Assessing how groups of people function and evolve as they seek to meet the needs of their members and of the organization ♦ *Interpersonal relationship building:* Effectively interacting with others in order to produce meaningful outcomes ♦ *Social awareness:* Seeing organizations as dynamic political, economic, and social systems
Determine the current level of commitment	♦ *Communication:* Applying effective verbal, nonverbal, and written communication methods to achieve desired results ♦ *Communication networks:* Understanding the various methods through which communication is achieved ♦ *Coping skills:* Dealing with ambiguity and stress resulting from conflicting information and goals; helping others deal with ambiguity and stress ♦ *Ethics modeling:* Modeling exemplary ethical behavior and understanding the implications of this responsibility ♦ *Group dynamics:* Assessing how groups of people function and evolve as they seek to meet the needs of their members and of the organization ♦ *Interpersonal relationship building:* Effectively interacting with others in order to produce meaningful outcomes ♦ *Social awareness:* Seeing organizations as dynamic political, economic, and social systems

(continued on next page)

Table 3.1: Relationship Between Analysis and the Competencies of the Analyst *(continued)*

Model of Analysis	Competencies of the Analyst
Assess the future environment	♦ *Ability to see the "big picture":* Identifying trends and patterns that are outside the normal paradigm of the organization ♦ *Identification of critical business issues:* Determining key business issues and forces for change and applying that knowledge to performance improvement strategies ♦ *Industry awareness:* Understanding the current and future climate of the organization's industry and formulating strategies that respond to that climate ♦ *Work environment analysis:* Examining the work environment for issues or characteristics that affect human performance; understanding characteristics of a high-performance workplace
Uncover the reasons for performance gaps	♦ *Performance theory:* Recognizing the implications, outcomes, and consequences of performance interventions to distinguish between activities and results ♦ *Systems thinking:* Recognizing the interrelationship among events by determining the driving forces that connect seemingly isolated incidents within the organization; taking a holistic view of performance problems in order to find root causes

Step 1: Determine the Current Performance Environment

Definition and Purpose of Step 1

Begin analysis by clarifying exactly where performance is being achieved (figure 3.2). Be clear about who is involved, what they do, how they do it, when they do it, what resources they use, and what others say about the results achieved.

The *performance environment* is like an onion: It has many layers. At the core is the individual; the first layer surrounding it is the work group or team; the second is the division or department; the third is the organization; the fourth is the national environment; and the fifth (the outermost) layer is the global environment. These layers are depicted in figure 3.3.

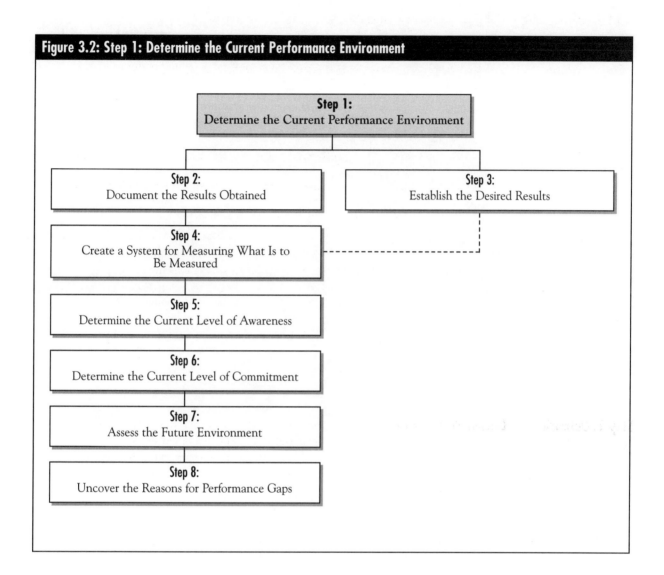

Figure 3.2: Step 1: Determine the Current Performance Environment

Step 1:
Determine the Current Performance Environment

Step 2:
Document the Results Obtained

Step 3:
Establish the Desired Results

Step 4:
Create a System for Measuring What Is to Be Measured

Step 5:
Determine the Current Level of Awareness

Step 6:
Determine the Current Level of Commitment

Step 7:
Assess the Future Environment

Step 8:
Uncover the Reasons for Performance Gaps

Figure 3.3: The Performance Environment

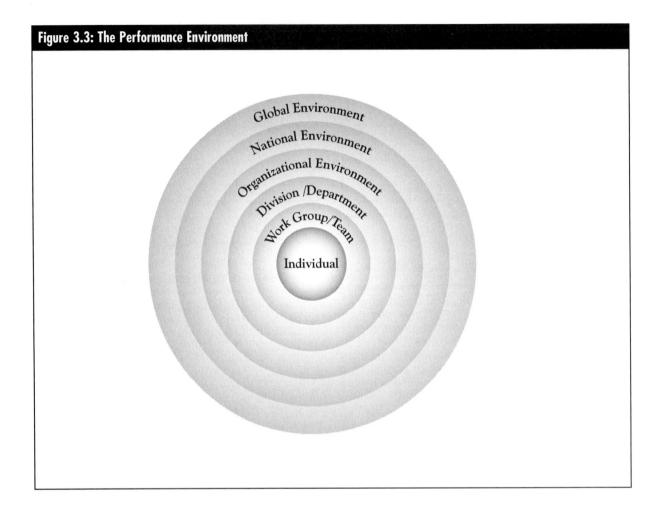

Global Environment
National Environment
Organizational Environment
Division /Department
Work Group/Team
Individual

The environment in which performance is being achieved is of utmost importance; indeed, W. Edwards Deming, known for his work with Total Quality, attributes as much as nine-tenths of all performance problems to the system or environment in which individuals must function, and only one-tenth to the individuals themselves (1986).

Examples of issues associated with the performance environment include:

♦ Status of the economy and of global competition

♦ The organization's strategic goals and objectives

♦ Top managers' ability to exercise leadership and guide the organization

♦ The organization's command structure and the way the work is organized into divisions or departments

♦ The department's goals and objectives

♦ Department managers' ability to exercise leadership

♦ The department's command structure and the way the work is organized into work units

♦ The work group's or team's goals and objectives

♦ The supervisor's ability to exercise leadership

♦ The work group's or team's command structure and the way the work is organized into jobs for individuals

♦ The individual's job duties and expectations.

Implementing Step 1

Begin by asking yourself, What is the performance environment? Conducting an organizational analysis, using such questions as the following, will help you find the answer.

- How clearly do people understand the performance that is expected of them, and how much agreement exists that such performance is desirable?

- How well can experienced performers recognize the situations in which they are expected to perform (that is, *identify performance cues*)?

- How often do people receive feedback on their performance? How clear is the feedback they receive? In what forms do they receive it?

- What tools, equipment, or other resources are essential to performance, and how many people have them when needed?

- How often do people confront decisions or situations for which they believe greater authority is needed? How often is access to that authority actually necessary? When necessary, how often is it available?

- How organized are work processes? Will good, experienced performers agree on these processes? Can the processes be diagrammed?

- In what ways are people provided with incentives for performing (before performance) and rewarded for performing (after performance)? Do they see what is in it for them?

- How much do people value the rewards they receive and believe that the performance required to achieve those rewards is fair, possible to be achieved, and will result in the promised rewards?

- Regarding new, possibly untried methods, how comfortable do performers feel about taking the risks to satisfy customers?

- How are people trained? How is their knowledge kept current?

- How are people recruited, selected, oriented, and advanced?

- How does the allocation of human resources follow work requirements and production cycles?

- How motivated are people to perform? How much do they want to achieve desired results?

Use the Step 1 section in the worksheet in figure 4.1 to pose these and related questions about the environment in which people perform. If you wish, poll employees on these and related issues using figure 3.4.

Step 1 is perhaps most important for external consultants, since they are especially in need of familiarizing themselves with the environment in which people are expected to carry out their work and achieve results.

Vignette: A large organization, the XYZ Corporation, was experiencing higher-than-average turnover. Chief Learning Officer Loretta Vasquez is asked by company management to examine the problem and find solutions. Vasquez hires Ronetta Brown, a seasoned external consultant, to help solve the problem. Brown begins by asking such questions as these:

- How are people hired into the system (inputs)?

- How are people treated while in the system (processes)?

- Why do people typically leave the organization, and where do they go (outputs)?

- What issues do current employees feel influence turnover?

- How much turnover is there in comparable organizations?

- What policies and procedures has the organization put in place that may affect turnover?

- What turnover is typical of organizations in the same industry and locale?

- What turnover is experienced by best-in-class organizations?

- What has been written on turnover, and what research has implications about turnover?

- What turnover is experienced by organizations that have established turnover reduction strategies?

- How should people be hired into the system (inputs)?

- How should people be treated while in the system (processes)?

Step 2: Document the Results Obtained

Definition and Purpose of Step 2

The second step of analysis is to clarify what is happening now, and what results are being obtained

Figure 3.4: Instrument for Assessing Employee Opinions About Performance Conditions

Directions: This instrument is designed to gauge your own opinions about performance conditions in the organization. For each statement below, circle a number to the right to indicate your level of agreement. Use the following scale:

1 = Strongly Disagree
2 = Disagree
3 = Agree
4 = Strongly Agree

When you finish scoring the instrument, hand it to the designated person and use it to pinpoint areas for performance improvement.

		Strongly Disagree			Strongly Agree
		1	2	3	4
1	I understand the performance expected of me.	1	2	3	4
2	I agree with the level of performance expected of me, since I think it is fair and equitable	1	2	3	4
3	I always know when to perform my duties.	1	2	3	4
4	I receive frequent, clear feedback about my performance.	1	2	3	4
5	My organization supplies me with the appropriate tools, equipment, and other resources I need to perform.	1	2	3	4
6	I have at hand the appropriate tools, equipment, and other resources available at the right time to help me when I need to perform.	1	2	3	4
7	I know what decisions I can make, and I know on what decisions I must obtain my supervisor's approval.	1	2	3	4
8	When I need my supervisor's approval, he or she is readily available to discuss it.	1	2	3	4
9	Work processes in this organization are well organized.	1	2	3	4
10	I am given adequate incentives to motivate me to perform.	1	2	3	4
11	I am given adequate rewards after I perform to make me want to continue to perform in accordance with performance expectations.	1	2	3	4
12	I value the rewards I receive.	1	2	3	4
13	I believe the performance targets that have been established for me are achievable.	1	2	3	4
14	I feel comfortable enough in this organization to risk making decisions to satisfy customers and achieve results through new, possibly untried, methods.	1	2	3	4

		Strongly Disagree			Strongly Agree
		1	2	3	4
15	I receive adequate training.	1	2	3	4
16	I believe that people are properly recruited for positions in this organization.	1	2	3	4
17	I believe that staff selection methods in this organization are effective in most cases in matching the right person with the right job.	1	2	3	4
18	People are properly oriented to their work in this organization.	1	2	3	4
19	People are given advancement opportunities in this organization that match their abilities.	1	2	3	4
20	I believe that scheduling of work in this organization is done effectively.	1	2	3	4
21	I believe that conditions in this organization are such that I feel motivated to perform at my peak.	1	2	3	4
	Scoring				

Directions: From the list of issues above, add up your scores from the right column and place the score in the shaded box appearing above. Identify the two issues with which you most agree and the two issues with which you least agree and list them below. Be prepared to discuss why you feel as you do and what you feel should be done to eliminate performance barriers in your organization.

Write your items here ➥

Issues With Which I Most Agree

	What Is the Issue?	Why Do You Feel That It Is an Issue? What Should Be Done to Remove the Issue as a Barrier to Performance?
1		
2		

Issues With Which I Least Agree

	What Is the Issue?	Why Do You Feel That It Is an Issue? What Should Be Done to Remove the Issue as a Barrier to Performance?
1		
2		

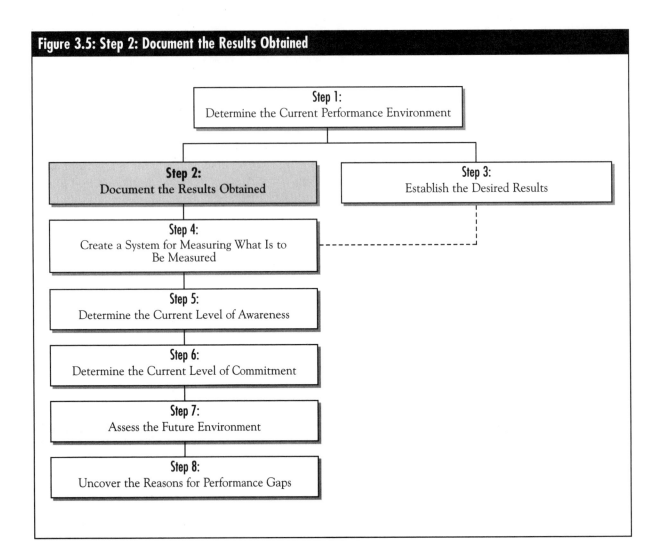

Figure 3.5: Step 2: Document the Results Obtained

Step 1:
Determine the Current Performance Environment

Step 2:
Document the Results Obtained

Step 3:
Establish the Desired Results

Step 4:
Create a System for Measuring What Is to Be Measured

Step 5:
Determine the Current Level of Awareness

Step 6:
Determine the Current Level of Commitment

Step 7:
Assess the Future Environment

Step 8:
Uncover the Reasons for Performance Gaps

(see figure 3.5). This step is necessary whenever you try to solve a problem; when you examine a work process to establish work responsibilities; when you attempt to formulate a business strategy; or when you assess an individual's performance.

Step 2 is the process of clarifying *condition*, defined as perceived events as they exist (Rothwell, 1996b). Examples of condition include:

♦ Sales records

♦ Information about customer satisfaction with the organization's products and services

♦ Information about employee satisfaction with the organization, as measured by attitude surveys or exit interviews of departing employees

♦ Production levels

♦ Scrap levels

♦ Quality reports, showing variations from norm

♦ Employee performance appraisals

♦ Number of union grievances filed

♦ Management or employee perceptions or opinions about what is and is not working well.

Implementing Step 2

To answer the question What results are being obtained? begin by collecting background information about the external environment, the organization, and the particular problem. Pose such questions as these:

- What is happening?

- Who is involved?

- How is the problem linked to the organization's business needs and strategic goals and objectives?

- How much is the problem costing the organization, and how is it measured?

- When did the problem first appear or become noticeable?

- Where is the problem most evident? Are there geographical variations in the severity of the problem?

- What steps have already been taken to solve the problem? What results have been obtained?

Whenever you encounter performance problems, use the Step 2 section in the worksheet in figure 4.1 to help pose these questions.

Collecting information about condition is the easiest part of the analyst's role; it is simply a matter of asking people what is happening at the moment and getting them to talk about the problem as they experience it.

Most people have no trouble doing that; they can discuss at length what their problems are, why those problems are important, what opportunities for improvement they believe might exist, and why those opportunities should be taken. When the performance problem has to do with the work that people do or the processes by which they do it, techniques like the DACUM method can often be a helpful starting point (see figure 3.6).

Vignette: Recall Step 1 in which the current situation at XYZ Corporation is a higher-than-average rate of turnover. Ronetta Brown, the consultant

---

Figure 3.6: The DACUM Process: A Powerful Tool for Achieving Improved Performance

What Is It?

DACUM is an acronym that stands for Developing a Curriculum. Robert Norton of Ohio State University developed it in the 1980s.

What Is It For?

DACUM provides detailed descriptions of activities performed on a daily basis by individuals in a given job category. It answers the question What do people do now? Answering that question is often helpful, since even experienced performers may do their work in different ways, depending on site or shift. Such differences can complicate recruitment, selection, orientation, training, transfer, job standards, and other employment actions.

How Does It Work?

To apply the DACUM process, carry out the following steps:

- *Step 1:* Target one occupational group or job category.

- *Step 2:* Select a panel of between eight and 12 exemplary ("star") performers from the group or job category to be examined, and two or three immediate exemplary organizational superiors of the targeted group.

- *Step 3:* Invite the panel to a session to focus attention on the details and responsibilities of the targeted group or job category.

- *Step 4:* Select a group facilitator and two assistant facilitators to conduct the session.

(continued on next page)

- *Step 5:* Assemble participants in a large room with a plain wall for a day or two.

- *Step 6:* Brief participants on the process and on job challenges they may face in the future.

- *Step 7:* Ask participants to list the functions or responsibilities and behaviors they perform.

- *Step 8:* Write the responses on sheets of paper and tape the sheets to the wall.

- *Step 9:* Continue the process until participants can no longer come up with any more functions, responsibilities, or behaviors.

- *Step 10:* Call a break.

- *Step 11:* Create exclusive categories in which to group the functions or responsibilities and behaviors.

- *Step 12:* Ask participants to return from break.

- *Step 13:* Verify the function/responsibility categories by asking participants to review them.

- *Step 14:* Make sure each of the functions or responsibilities and behaviors that the participants have identified is assigned to the proper category and is not revised, deleted (because other function/responsibilities overlap with it), or that no more functions are added to the list (because they were initially forgotten).

- *Step 15:* Call another break.

- *Step 16:* Place function/responsibility categories and behaviors in an order based on what a newcomer needs to learn the job (i.e., by difficulty to learn, by prerequisite task, by ease of learning, etc.).

- *Step 17:* Ask participants to return from break to verify and/or modify the order.

- *Step 18:* Adjourn the meeting.

- *Step 19:* Remove the chart from the wall and have it typed.

- *Step 20:* Circulate copies of the chart among the participants for review in the form described in Step 21.

- *Step 21:* Prepare surveys to identify work roles, outputs, competencies, quality requirements, future trends, and ethical challenges related to each function or responsibility and behavior appearing on the chart.

- *Step 22:* Conduct the surveys, compile results, and present the results for review to another group of exemplary job incumbents and their immediate supervisors as a form of validation to double-check the opinions of these groups about the results of the surveys.

What Are the Results?

The result of the DACUM process is a *validated job model* based on the views of exemplary performers. It is much more detailed than a job description, and it reflects what people say they actually do, rather than what others say they do or what others say they *should* do.

Since a DACUM chart describes only what people do and not what they should do, it can be an immensely valuable tool to help bring common understanding to what people do in their work. By comparing a DACUM chart to a manufacturing flowchart, for instance, it can demonstrate differences between what the engineers say people should be doing on the assembly line and what they are actually doing.

How Can the DACUM Chart Be Used?

Once the DACUM chart has been prepared and checked and double-checked, it can be transformed easily into a check sheet to guide planned on-the-job training based on how exemplary performers think training can be conducted. Using a job model that these performers have developed grounds the chart in the reality of the work and gains the support of the best workers to use it and apply it.

A DACUM chart can be the foundation for subsequent work-related issues. Additional research based on a DACUM chart can be a way to clarify:

♦ *Entry-level knowledge:* Since the DACUM chart spells out what people do, it can also provide a starting point for determining what people should know at entry level.

♦ *Employee recruitment and selection:* By clarifying what people do, the DACUM chart can become a starting point for developing skills tests and refining interview and selection protocols.

♦ *Work standards:* Each cell of a DACUM chart identifies a work activity. Intensive follow-up work is needed to extend the identification of work activities to the next step, which is clarification of the results of those work activities.

♦ *Career paths:* When a DACUM chart for a job category is compared to charts for high levels of the same category or different but parallel categories, people can learn what they need to move from their present position to any other.

♦ *Training:* By clarifying and identifying what people do, the DACUM chart can become a starting point for focusing attention on job-specific training needs.

♦ *Work process improvement:* As a snapshot of how the work is being done, the DACUM chart can become a starting point for focusing attention on how the work is performed, and how it should be performed.

♦ *Employee performance appraisal:* By clarifying and identifying what people do, the DACUM chart can become a starting point for providing job-specific feedback to people about their performance.

♦ *Reward systems:* By clarifying and identifying what people do, the DACUM chart can become a starting point for determining how well people are rewarded for how they perform.

What Are the Merits of DACUM?

DACUM is:

♦ fast

♦ a process that involves experienced workers and management, thus providing "ownership" of the process

♦ a means of clarifying work expectations and responsibilities—the lack of which is a common cause of performance problems

♦ able to produce an immediate "deliverable"—that is, a check sheet to guide on-the-job training

♦ a starting point for uncovering specific issues or activities for which some disagreement exists.

What Are the Drawbacks of DACUM?

DACUM:

♦ requires time away from work for "best-in-class" performers, thereby necessitating management commitment due to lost production

♦ does not work well when there is only one employee in a given job category

♦ does not work well when production processes are undergoing change

♦ does not work well unless management commits itself strongly to following through on using the results.

hired to investigate the performance problem, begins by asking questions to gauge turnover and treatment issues as outlined in Step 1. Taking a pulse of how turnover varies by work units and geographic regions, consequences of high turnover, hiring practices, and how employees are treated helped Brown focus her initial analysis efforts.

Step 3: Establish the Desired Results

Definition and Purpose of Step 3

The analyst's third step is to determine the results that are desired or optimal; these are called *criteria* (see figure 3.7). Examples include:

♦ Organizational policy

♦ Organizational procedures

♦ Customer expectations, either explicitly stated or derived implicitly from practice

♦ Industry practice

♦ Best practice

♦ Laws, regulations, ordinances

♦ Management values or expectations

♦ Vision statement

♦ Job descriptions

♦ Collective bargaining agreements

♦ Work standards or expectations

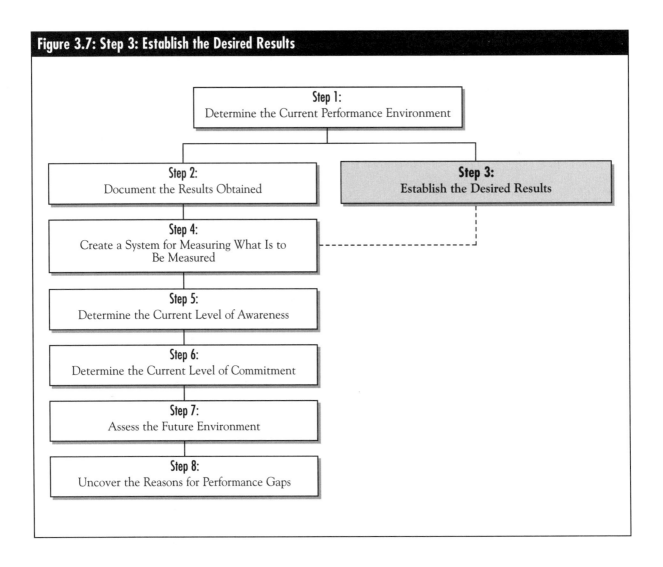

Figure 3.7: Step 3: Establish the Desired Results

Step 1:
Determine the Current Performance Environment

Step 2:
Document the Results Obtained

Step 3:
Establish the Desired Results

Step 4:
Create a System for Measuring What Is to Be Measured

Step 5:
Determine the Current Level of Awareness

Step 6:
Determine the Current Level of Commitment

Step 7:
Assess the Future Environment

Step 8:
Uncover the Reasons for Performance Gaps

- Productivity levels of the best performers (*exemplars*).

Each of these criteria focuses on desirable or optimal practice—ideals to be achieved—rather than on actual or current practice.

In many cases, clarifying criteria can be helpful in its own right, and can serve as a human performance improvement intervention. In other words, analysts sometimes discover that stakeholders, decision makers, or other interested parties do not share a common understanding of (or are at least not necessarily in agreement about) desirable results. Often, simply drawing attention to such differences of opinion can prompt meaningful dialogue, or *appreciative inquiry* (Barrett, 1995), into desired results and the best approaches by which to achieve them.

Implementing Step 3

To answer the question What results are desired? ask yourself the following:

For determining desired results

- What issues or trends in the work environment call for new action? Where are competitive conditions headed, and why?

- What are the performance differences among the best-performing organizations in the industry, and how does the performance of these organizations (as judged by return on equity or other measures) compare to that of the organization in which you are conducting your analysis?

- What are the differences between the highest-performing and the lowest-performing work units? Individuals? What accounts for those differences?

- How should the organization provide guidance to performers about what is expected of them? How should disagreements be resolved?

- What key business issues are affecting the organization? Which ones are most important, and why?

- How profitable is the organization at the present time? How profitable should it be in the future? What are the goals for profitability?

- What are the return on investment (ROI) and return on equity (ROE) that the organization is currently realizing? What are the organization's goals for ROI and ROE? (If it is a large organization, which of its parts are realizing the greatest ROI and ROE, and why are those parts more successful than others?)

- What is the organization's targeted market share? How was that target established? How realistic is it?

- What are the targets for quality? What error rates have been targeted? How realistic are those targets? Have they ever been achieved?

- What are the targets for customer satisfaction? How have they been identified, measured, and tracked? What feedback is given by whom about customer satisfaction to performers? How much should they be receiving?

- What should be happening? What results or outcomes are desired?

- Who should be involved to make that happen?

- How will realization of the goal help meet the organization's business needs and achieve strategic goals and objectives?

- When (over what time span) are the desired results to be achieved?

- What are the interim goals, or milestones, that can be achieved toward realization of the ultimate goal?

- What will the optimal state look like? What will be happening when it is achieved? What results will be obtained?

- What steps have already been taken to create a vision or to spell out the desired results? What level of agreement has been reached on them among decision makers?

Use the Step 3 section in the worksheet in figure 4.1 to help pose these questions.

Vignette: Continuing with the situation set up in Steps 1 and 2, Ronetta Brown proceeds to gather information about desired or optimal results from the XYZ Corporation's human resources department and from numerous managers. Toward that end, she asks her company-assigned liaison and several other people in the organization to tell her what approaches to collecting data seem to have worked best in the context of their corporate culture. Her informants suggest that she email the managers with her questions. They also suggest that before she does so, the liaison advise the managers by email that she will be approaching them.

These are some of the questions she then poses, thereby clarifying the desired situation by creating criteria against which comparisons can be made:

♦ How much turnover do the organization's decision makers feel to be tolerable (even desirable)?

♦ How much should turnover vary by geographical area, work unit, or division? What differences might exist by area, unit, or division?

♦ What (if anything) do the decision makers think might be the benefits of turnover?

Step 4: Create a System for Measuring What Is to Be Measured

Definition and Purpose of Step 4

As noted earlier, a performance gap is the disparity between the results that are being obtained and those that are desired. While perceptions by management and employees about performance gaps are important, perceptions vary and are not entirely reliable. When perceptions are unreliable, or when decision makers have unrealistic expectations, it may be necessary to shape more realistic ones. That might include benchmarking best practices or common practices, querying customers, or assembling stakeholders for a discussion of actual and desired measurement methods or output levels.

If, by contrast, a performance gap can be measured and documented, its impact on results determined, and the difference between actual and ideal demonstrated (see figure 3.8), then this difference should create an *impetus for change*—a desire to move away from the status quo toward solutions to problems.

There are two general kinds of performance gaps: hard and soft.

Hard performance gaps are those that lend themselves to measurement—for example, falling production figures, rising accident rates, or declining

sales. The causes of such gaps may be elusive, but the facts are indisputable and relatively easy to assess.

Soft performance gaps, by contrast, are those that are not easily subjected to measurement. When managers or employees complain of a morale problem or a communication problem, when they contend that customer service is "not what it should be," when decision makers or stakeholders feel there is a discrepancy between what they think ought to be happening and what *is* happening—in other words, when what the analyst confronts seems to be more a matter of perception than of data—then we are in the realm of soft performance gaps. They fill the lives of many managers and analysts with anxiety and both managers and analysts alike are plagued by them.

For years, Bob Mager referred to the vague terms that managers or employees use in describing soft performance gaps as *warm fuzzies*. These are complaints that at first sound clear, but in fact are not at all; they are open to interpretation and debate. For instance, what does it really mean to say that "communication in the company is not what it should be and needs to be improved"? Similar such pronouncements include:

♦ "Our employees haven't been trained well enough."

♦ "We don't function like a team in this company."

♦ "People in this organization aren't adequately rewarded for their effort."

♦ "We have too much red tape."

♦ "Our production processes are full of bottlenecks."

♦ "Employee morale is really bad."

Each of these comments qualifies as a "fuzzy," or an *implied performance gap*. Each sounds reasonable and may be difficult to refute, but it has no clear or specific meaning. Each can be interpreted differently by different listeners.

What is also unclear in the case of the "fuzzy" is how the speaker arrived at his or her conclusion—on what information that conclusion was based. It falls to the analyst to determine the answer.

"Fuzzies" show up as recommendations, solutions, or performance improvement strategies to problems that in fact have never really been identified. For instance, a manager might say:

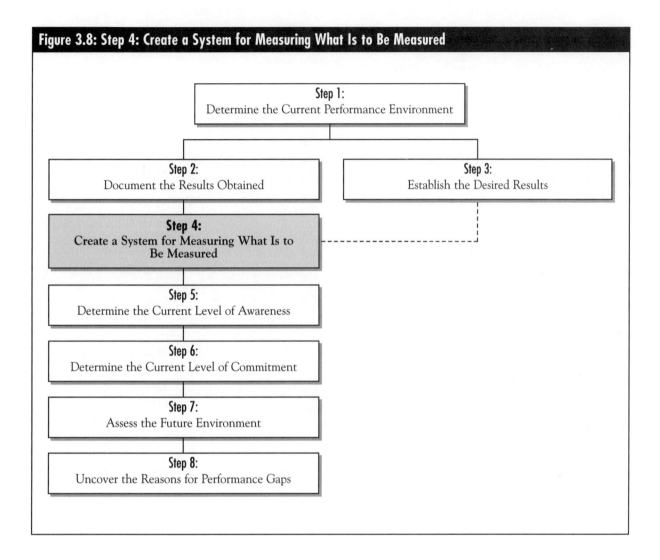

Figure 3.8: Step 4: Create a System for Measuring What Is to Be Measured

Step 1:
Determine the Current Performance Environment

Step 2:
Document the Results Obtained

Step 3:
Establish the Desired Results

Step 4:
Create a System for Measuring What Is to Be Measured

Step 5:
Determine the Current Level of Awareness

Step 6:
Determine the Current Level of Commitment

Step 7:
Assess the Future Environment

Step 8:
Uncover the Reasons for Performance Gaps

♦ "We need to offer a writing course."

♦ "We should increase our pay scale."

♦ "Let's conduct an attitude survey."

♦ "We need to look at our disciplinary and termination policies."

Again it is up to the analyst to unravel the mystery: It is necessary to backtrack, to compare the results that are being achieved with the results that are desired, and to determine what measurable gap exists between them.

Implementing Step 4

Analysts cannot properly diagnose a problem if the problem is couched in vague pronouncements like

those above. By insisting that a gap be made measurable, the analyst elicits what facts must be investigated, assesses the degree to which they may be controversial, and begins to zero in on appropriate actions or strategies for closing (or at least diminishing) the gap. It is hard work.

To measure a hard performance gap, on the other hand, the analyst has merely to identify sources of information (for example, documents or records; for possible sources, see figure 3.9), collect the information, organize it, examine it, draw conclusions from it, and verify the conclusions with knowledgeable people inside or outside the organization. (Some sources of information about soft performance gaps—the starting points for making soft gaps measurable—appear in figure 3.10.)

Figure 3.9: Sources of Information About Hard Performance Gaps

Output Measures

- Items Manufactured
- Number of People Served
- Products Sold
- Activities Completed
- Number of Items Shipped
- Products Assembled per Hour
- New Customers Identified
- Customers Retained

Time Measures

- Time Required for Training
- Labor Time
- Down Time
- Length of Order Response
- Time to Process Orders
- Time to Ship Orders
- Time to Serve Customers
- Waiting Time for Customers

Cost Measures

- Fixed Cost
- Variable Cost
- Overhead Expense
- Labor Cost
- Fringe Benefit Costs per Labor Hour
- Workers' Compensation

Quality Measures

- Product Rejects
- Customer Satisfaction
- Products Returned
- Products Rejected
- Scrap Rates
- Sales Not Completed

Figure 3.10: Sources of Information About Soft Performance Gaps

Work Habits

- Average time at lunch
- Average time at break
- Complaints about supervisors or employees

Suggestions and Innovations

- Suggestions filed
- Suggestions accepted
- Savings based on suggestions

Worker Satisfaction/Morale

- Absenteeism
- Tardiness
- Avoidable turnover
- Union grievances
- Employee ratings in questionnaires upon exit interview
- Employee ratings in attitude surveys

Employee Development

- Number of employees who have completed probation successfully
- Number of employees certified upon successful demonstration of competency by job certification
- Amount of payroll invested in training
- Amount of work time devoted to training
- Amount of money spent on tuition reimbursement

But usually the analyst must first apply what Mager calls *goal analysis*—the function of which, he says, is "to define the indefinable, to tangibilitate the intangible—to help us say what we mean by our important but abstract goals (or *fuzzies*, as they will be called in this book). With this procedure, it is possible to describe the essential elements of abstract states—to identify the main performances that go to make up the meaning of the goal" (1972, page 10).

To apply goal analysis, the analyst must first of all understand whether the performance gap with which he or she has been confronted is hard or soft. If soft, the analyst should pose such questions as these:

♦ What would people be doing if they were performing in line with the desired goal?

♦ What measurable results would occur?

♦ How would you know this when you see it? Describe exactly what would be happening when people are performing in this way.

The observable behaviors are listed and then reported to managers as a starting point for developing a clear, specific, and measurable description of what behaviors are linked to the *fuzzy*.

For example, the analyst might ask customers how often they observe certain behaviors and how they react to them. The analyst can then estimate the value of sales that have been lost as a result of negative customer reaction. Having a figure for the value of the performance to be improved can be useful in demonstrating the need for performance intervention strategies (Swanson, 1988).

To cite another example, suppose a manager complains that employees "are not demonstrating an appropriate attitude toward customer service." The phrase "attitude toward customer service" is a fuzzy: Having an ideal state in mind, the manager has implied that there is a performance gap, but exactly what the ideal state would look like is not apparent.

To help define the manager's ideal vision and thus shed light on the degree to which the actual situation falls short, the analyst applies goal analysis—for example, asking managers to list whatever behaviors they associate with good customer service, what behaviors they associate with poor customer service,

and how often they spot each. The manager is then in a better position to estimate the value of lost business attributable to the bad behaviors.

To initiate goal analysis, refer to figure 3.11. (The same approach can be effectively used with teams or focus groups.) While most commonly applied to training problems, goal analysis lends itself to other applications as well.

Vignette: Once again, consider the turnover problem. Suppose that Ronetta Brown has determined that turnover at XYZ Corporation is 10 percent, up from 6 percent a year before. Suppose further that the average salary of persons voluntarily leaving the organization is $30,000, and that 20 people have left in the past year. Next, suppose it takes a year's training before a replacement worker is in a position to perform at or above the level of an experienced worker.

Given these suppositions, turnover at XYZ Corporation is in effect costing eight more people than are actually leaving.

The theoretical cost of training the replacements would thus be $240,000 for the year (eight people at an annual salary of $30,000 each).

However, these replacements are not altogether unproductive. Suppose their collective productivity during training is worth $50,000. In other words, the estimated cost of the performance problem is $240,000 minus $50,000, or $190,000. That is still a sizable amount that could be saved by reducing turnover.

Vignette: Suppose manager Laura Anderson remarks to WLP practitioner Ron Evans that the organization "needs to offer customer service training."

This too is the kind of statement that calls for a human performance improvement intervention, since it comes at the end of a chain of thinking to which the WLP practitioner is not privy: It is not clear why Anderson believes such intervention is warranted, what facts or interpretations underlie her request, how many people would be affected, what behavior is desired, what gap exists, or how the gap might be measured.

If Evans responds to Anderson simply by asking when the training will be needed, he is unlikely to solve the real problem.

Figure 3.11: Worksheet for Conducting Goal Analysis

Directions: Use this worksheet to help you, as analyst, conduct goal analysis when a "fuzzy" is used by a manager, employee, customer, or other stakeholder. In the space below, describe the "fuzzy." Then pose the questions about it to the individual or group who used the term. The idea of goal analysis is to clarify otherwise vague pronouncements.

1	What is the "fuzzy" that was used?
2	What would people be doing when they are performing in accordance with the desired goal? (List.)
3	What measurable results would result from this behavior? (List.)
4	How do you know this behavior is in accordance with desired goals when you see it? Describe exactly what will be happening when people are performing in this way.

The appropriate response, rather, would be to help Anderson appreciate the range of variables that may be inhibiting performance. Evans would use such questions as:

♦ What has prompted the manager to call for intervention now?

♦ What results are presently being obtained? (What is happening now?)

♦ What results are desired? What standards, if any, exist to measure the quality of customer service, and how are they applied?

♦ What is the measurable gap (the difference between actual and desired results)?

♦ What is the estimated cost of that gap?

♦ If no action is taken, what will be the cost of the gap to the organization over the next year? In the course of the next five years?

Evans will then ask what solutions Anderson has already tried, what results stemmed from those efforts, and what other ideas she may have explored to address the problem.

Once again, one of the analyst's goals is to make the problem measurable in terms of cost to the organization. Since there are limitations on time, people, and money, care must be taken to focus organizational priorities only on those issues that will have a measurable payoff.

Think of it, in other words, as a favorable return on investment. Deciding to take action is in effect an investment decision, and it should be treated with the same prudence as any other investment decision.

Use the Step 4 section in the worksheet in figure 4.1 to organize your thinking about how to make problems measurable.

Step 5: Determine the Current Level of Awareness

Definition and Purpose of Step 5

Usually it is only when people become aware of a performance gap that they are willing to make changes. Hence, assessing awareness levels (and building awareness when it is lacking) is an important step in the analytic process (see figure 3.12).

In terms of awareness, organizational problems fall into four general categories, which are represented in figure 3.13. For any problem you face, think about

where the problem falls on the grid, and what efforts on the analyst's part might shift it to another location.

The first problem category, found in cell 1 of the grid, consists of matters about which people are keenly aware and may have strong feelings. Finding an audience of eager listeners is not difficult (including decision makers, who are willing to hear out anyone who has ideas about how to solve the problem). In a classic example, the organization is on the verge of bankruptcy.

The second category is one in which people are also aware of the problem, but do not care much about it; they are too pressed by other issues to give it their immediate attention. Even when decision makers acknowledge the problem's importance, they feel they need to devote more of their time and resources to matters they regard as more central to their day-to-day need to get work out and keep cash coming in. A typical example of this category, at least for some organizations, is the question of succession planning.

The third category is one in which people are unaware of a problem, but would probably care if they knew of it. Examples that might fall into this category include replacement technologies, new work methods adopted by cutting-edge organizations, and new applications of management theory. (A simple example is the current growth of electronic commerce. While just a few years ago unnoticed by many managers, recently "e-commerce" has begun to command an enormous amount of attention and interest. The problem for newcomers is that the pioneers enjoy the advantage of having been there first.)

The fourth category, about which little needs to be said, consists of problems about which people are unaware and would not care even if they were.

Implementing Step 5

The easiest problems for an analyst to address are those about which people both know and care, since a constituency already exists to solve them. While certain obvious crises fall into this category, the analyst's challenge is that decision makers often want quick results. The analyst must try to channel that sense of urgency into effective strategies, rather than ill-considered actions that could do more harm than good.

The most difficult problem for the analyst to handle is the type of which people are unaware but in fact would care about if they knew more. Unorganized

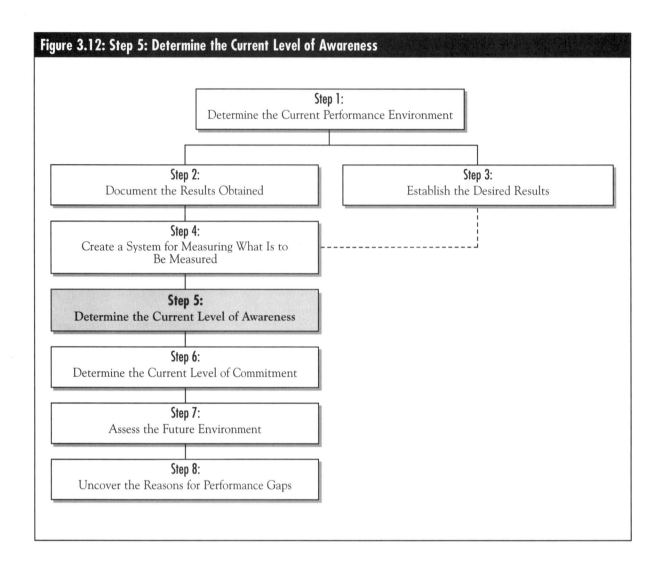

Figure 3.12: Step 5: Determine the Current Level of Awareness

Step 1:
Determine the Current Performance Environment

Step 2:
Document the Results Obtained

Step 3:
Establish the Desired Results

Step 4:
Create a System for Measuring What Is to Be Measured

Step 5:
Determine the Current Level of Awareness

Step 6:
Determine the Current Level of Commitment

Step 7:
Assess the Future Environment

Step 8:
Uncover the Reasons for Performance Gaps

on-the-job training is a typical example. Instead of a planned training program, a new hire is merely told to "follow Joe around the plant" or "sit by Mary and watch what she does."

A substantial body of research and practice, dating from World War II, suggests that in fact organizations can achieve measurable payoffs by investing in planned on-the-job training—measurable, that is, by comparing the time (translatable as salary) that it takes to help a worker reach full productivity using planned (as opposed to unplanned) training. Yet in many organizations decision makers either do not know of the concept of planned training or are ignorant as to how they might institute it.

It is the analyst's job to identify and draw attention to *all* problems. When the payoff will be great from tackling a problem about which people are

unaware but that the analyst has determined they would care about if they knew, it is especially important that the analyst make them aware. That can be done by the following means:

♦ Preparing a white paper for management that pinpoints problems and lays out the case for addressing them

♦ Approaching potential champions or sponsors of change—people who might be willing, for example, to pilot-test performance improvement interventions

♦ Holding briefing sessions for management or other interested parties

♦ Circulating memos (or email) about the problems

Figure 3.13: Grid to Assess Awareness

	Awareness	
	High	**Low**
Care High	**Cell 1** People are aware and care about the problem.	**Cell 3** People are not aware but would care about the problem if they only knew about it.
Care Low	**Cell 2** People are aware but care more about other problems.	**Cell 4** People are not aware and would not care about the problem.

♦ Asking questions that draw attention to a problem; people feel they "own" a problem or solution that they have "discovered" on their own

♦ Calling in outside speakers to address management audiences.

Vignette: Ronetta Brown wants to gauge awareness about turnover in the corporation. Toward that end, she approaches several people: the company president, the vice president for human resources, a union leader, and several hourly workers. Among the questions she poses are these:

♦ How do you define turnover? Tell me what it is and what it is not. Is termination an example of turnover? Is retirement? Is death? Is promotion from one department to another?

♦ What consequences have you personally observed that stemmed from turnover?

♦ What consequences to customer service do you believe have stemmed from turnover?

♦ What price tag would you attribute to turnover in the organization?

From the answers to these questions, Brown may learn that her respondents are aware of the issue of turnover, agree uniformly that it is a problem, and point to higher-than-necessary overtime as one of its consequences.

Use the Step 5 section in the worksheet in figure 4.1 to organize your thinking on how to determine the current level of awareness.

Step 6: Determine the Current Level of Commitment

Definition and Purpose of Step 6

Awareness, whether preexisting or fostered by the analyst, is not the same thing as *commitment*—a concept that answers the question How much perceived need exists to take action to solve a problem?

(see figure 3.14). Awareness without commitment does not lead to action and consigns the issue to the second category of the awareness grid: those problems about which people are aware but do not care much about.

Implementing Step 6

As noted earlier, the surest way to test commitment to solving a problem is to request the resources to solve it. Working alone or with a team of interested stakeholders, the analyst prepares an action plan that should at least include:

♦ Description of the problem to be addressed

♦ Estimate of the cost and value of the problem to the organization

♦ Explanation of how that estimate was derived

♦ Statement of the need for further investigation

♦ Step-by-step action plan to further investigate the problem, including descriptions of who will be involved and what results will be obtained from each task

♦ A timeline showing how long it will take to carry out the analysis

♦ A budget for the project

♦ A description of the staff needed to conduct the project.

Use the "Worksheet for Organizing a Proposal" (figure 3.15) to implement this step. If the proposal you develop is accepted, you could have an indication

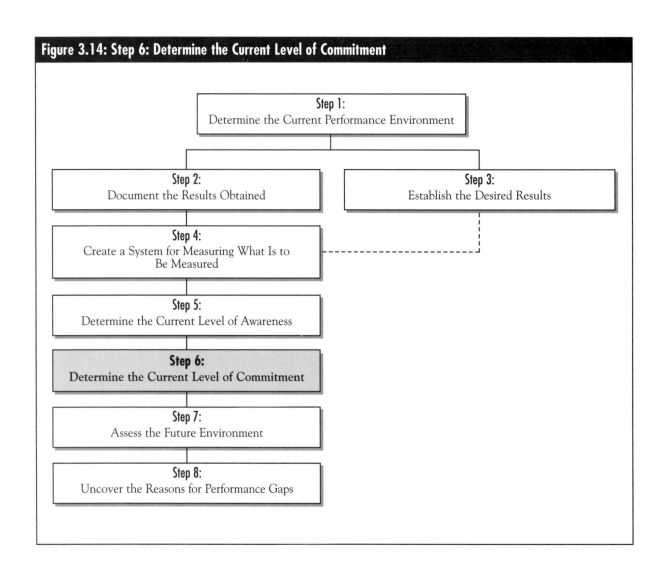

Figure 3.14: Step 6: Determine the Current Level of Commitment

Step 1:
Determine the Current Performance Environment

Step 2:
Document the Results Obtained

Step 3:
Establish the Desired Results

Step 4:
Create a System for Measuring What Is to Be Measured

Step 5:
Determine the Current Level of Awareness

Step 6:
Determine the Current Level of Commitment

Step 7:
Assess the Future Environment

Step 8:
Uncover the Reasons for Performance Gaps

(although not a foolproof one) that the organization's decision makers are committed to taking action. If the decision makers allot substantial resources to implementing the proposal, you have a still stronger indication of commitment. The highest possible level of commitment is demonstrated when decision makers offer to participate personally in the project.

You can rate the level of awareness and commitment to address a specific performance problem by using the questionnaires in figures 3.16 and 3.17 and score evaluations in figure 3.18. Use the Step 6 section in the worksheet in figure 4.1 to pose your questions about the current level of commitment.

Vignette: Ronetta Brown, the analyst, decides to gauge the level of commitment to addressing the perceived problem of excessive turnover. The majority of respondents say that turnover is "to be expected, since pay rates are low." From that, Brown infers that there is little commitment to addressing the problem.

However, using information gathered in other steps, she hypothesizes that turnover could be addressed through means other than by increasing compensation. She then researches turnover reduction strategies in the rest of the industry and drafts a detailed proposal for a pilot test that should help determine whether another possible performance improvement intervention—in particular, launching a mentoring and socialization program—might help reduce turnover. A mentoring program, of course, would link each newcomer to more knowledgeable and experienced workers, while a socialization program would help people adapt to the corporate culture. She presents the results of her analysis and proposal to her client and several other managers known for their willingness to experiment with new ideas and approaches.

After a low-profile pilot test of the strategy, Brown is able to demonstrate that turnover reduction would indeed be possible. At this point she proposes the intervention to top managers.

Figure 3.15: Worksheet for Organizing a Proposal

Directions: Use this worksheet to organize a proposal for conducting an analysis project. For each question appearing below, provide information. (Use additional paper as needed.)

1	What is the problem to be addressed?
2	What is the estimate of the cost or value of the problem to the organization? Why is it important? How was the estimate determined?
3	How can the problem be investigated?
4	What step-by-step action plan is being proposed to investigate the problem? Who should be involved? What results or deliverables should be obtained from each step? (Include milestones or deliverables for each step.)
5	What is the project timeline? How long will it take to carry out? (Show timeline in relation to steps.)
6	What is the estimated budget for the project?
7	Who will be needed to conduct the project? Why will they be needed?

Figure 3.16: Instrument for Measuring Awareness of a Performance Problem

Directions: Use this instrument to measure the awareness of the performance problem. For each statement below, circle a number to the right indicating how much you perceive the issue to be a problem. Use the following scale:

1 = Strongly Disagree
2 = Disagree
3 = Agree
4 = Strongly Agree

When you finish scoring, refer to the evaluation section at the end of the instrument..

Awareness of the Problem	Strongly Disagree			Strongly Agree
	1	2	3	4
1 Top managers in the organization are generally not aware of the problem.	1	2	3	4
2 Middle managers in the organization are generally not aware of the problem.	1	2	3	4
3 Supervisors in the organization are generally not aware of the problem.	1	2	3	4
4 Workers in the organization are generally not aware of the problem.	1	2	3	4
5 Top managers in the organization are generally not aware of the problem's impact on the organization.	1	2	3	4
6 Middle managers in the organization are generally not aware of the problem's impact on the organization.	1	2	3	4
7 Supervisors in the organization are generally not aware of the problem's impact on the organization.	1	2	3	4
8 Workers in the organization are generally not aware of the problem's impact on the organization.	1	2	3	4
Add up the scores from columns 1 through 8 and insert the sum at right:				

Figure 3.17: Instrument for Measuring Commitment to Solving a Performance Problem

Directions: Use this instrument to measure the commitment to solving a performance problem. For each statement below, circle a number to the right indicating how much you perceive the commitment to be. Use the following scale:

$$1 = \text{Strongly Disagree}$$
$$2 = \text{Disagree}$$
$$3 = \text{Agree}$$
$$4 = \text{Strongly Agree}$$

When you finish scoring, refer to the evaluation section at the end of the instrument.

Commitment to Action	Strongly Disagree			Strongly Agree
	1	2	3	4
1 Judging by what they say, top managers in the organization are generally not committed to taking action to solve the problem.	1	2	3	4
2 Judging by what they say, middle managers in the organization are generally not committed to taking action to solve the problem.	1	2	3	4
3 Judging by what they say, supervisors in the organization are generally not committed to taking action to solve the problem.	1	2	3	4
4 Judging by what they say, workers in the organization are generally not committed to taking action to solve the problem.	1	2	3	4
5 Judging by their unwillingness to devote time, money, or personal attention to the problem, top managers in the organization are generally not committed to taking action to solve the problem.	1	2	3	4
6 Judging by their unwillingness to devote time, money, or personal attention to the problem, middle managers in the organization are generally not committed to taking action to solve the problem.	1	2	3	4
7 Judging by their unwillingness to devote time, money, or personal attention to the problem, supervisors in the organization are generally not committed to taking action to solve the problem.	1	2	3	4
8 Judging by their unwillingness to devote time, money, or personal attention to the problem, workers in the organization are generally not committed to taking action to solve the problem.	1	2	3	4
Add up the scores from columns 1 through 8 and insert the sum at right:				

Figure 3.18: Score Evaluations for Awareness and Commitment Instruments

Score Evaluation for Awareness Instrument

If your score was between 8 and 16, then: Key groups in your organization have high awareness about the human performance problem. You need take no action to build awareness.

If your score was between 17 and 32, then: Key groups in your organization have some awareness of the human performance problem. You should take some steps to increase awareness.

If your score was 33 or greater, then: Key groups in your organization have low awareness of the human performance problem. You need to take many steps to increase awareness.

Score Evaluation for Commitment Instrument

If your score was between 8 and 16, then: Key groups in your organization have high commitment to solving the human performance problem. You need take no action to build commitment.

If your score was between 17 and 32, then: Key groups in your organization have moderate commitment to solving the human performance problem. You need take no action to build commitment.

If your score was 33 or greater, then: Key groups in your organization have low commitment to solving the human performance problem. You need to take many steps to increase commitment.

NOTE:

♦ A high score on the awareness instrument indicates that people in the organization know about the performance problem.

♦ A high score on the commitment instrument indicates that people in the organization are committed to solving the problem.

♦ A low score on the awareness instrument but a high score on the commitment instrument indicates that there is a great willingness to take action, but a limited awareness of the problem.

♦ A high score on the awareness instrument but a low score on the commitment instrument indicates that there is much awareness of the problem, but limited enthusiasm for taking corrective action.

Step 7: Assess the Future Environment

Definition and Purpose of Step 7

Human performance problems are not static; like everything else in today's world, change is the only constant. Thus an important question to consider in addressing performance problems is How is the gap likely to change in the future? (See figure 3.19.)

Implementing Step 7

To carry out Step 7, an analyst uses *environmental scanning*—the process of examining an organization's external environment and identifying trends that may influence the performance of the organization, work group, or individual in the future (unlike Step 1, which focuses on the current performance environment). Environmental scanning helps the analyst

establish and maintain a proactive stance, anticipating and possibly averting performance problems before they arise.

Environmental monitoring for WLP is the same as environmental scanning for HRD (Rothwell and Kazanas, 1994). In it, the analyst:

♦ classifies the external environment into sectors (A sector is a portion of the world outside the organization that is categorized into a discrete component for separate analysis.)

♦ determines an appropriate time horizon

♦ examines the sectors for expected changes over the proposed time horizon

♦ infers the effects of environmental changes on (a) the general public; (b) external stakeholders; (c) departments or work groups in the organiza-

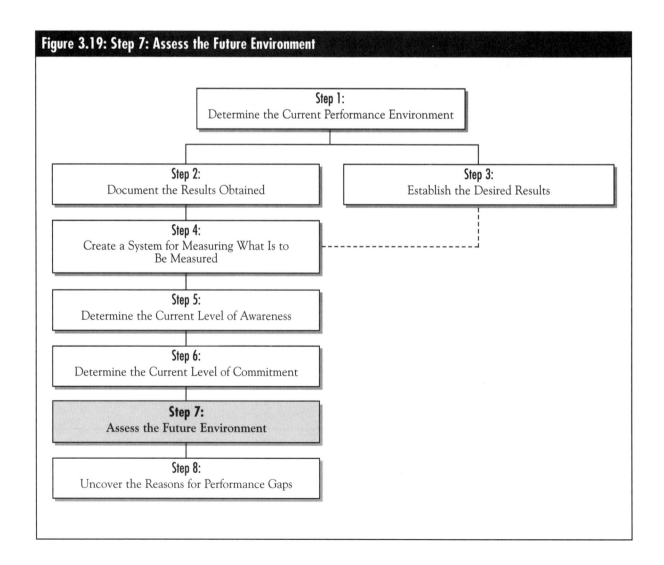

Figure 3.19: Step 7: Assess the Future Environment

Step 1:
Determine the Current Performance Environment

Step 2:
Document the Results Obtained

Step 3:
Establish the Desired Results

Step 4:
Create a System for Measuring What Is to Be Measured

Step 5:
Determine the Current Level of Awareness

Step 6:
Determine the Current Level of Commitment

Step 7:
Assess the Future Environment

Step 8:
Uncover the Reasons for Performance Gaps

tion; (d) individuals in the organization; and (e) job or work requirements

♦ infers the effects of environmental changes as they may affect workplace learning and performance in the organization and in each work group

♦ pinpoints possible future threats or opportunities created by trends and mounts performance improvement interventions either to avert the threats or seize the opportunities, as the case may be.

These steps (referred to as 7A-7F) are illustrated in figure 3.20. Use the Step 7 section in the worksheet in figure 4.1 to guide you through these 7A-7F steps. The placement of environmental scanning within the analysis process is diagrammed in figure 3.21.

There are many sectors into which the external environment can be subdivided for monitoring (step 7A). Sectors include:

♦ *Economic conditions*—that is, conditions having to do with the business cycle and the relative climate for the organization in a nation, region, or globally, including preferences of both individual and institutional consumers

♦ *Political conditions*—that is, having to do with the relative climate that politics creates for the organization in a nation, region, or globally

♦ *Legal/regulatory conditions*—that is, having to do with laws, regulations, and rules affecting the organization in a nation, region, or globally

♦ *Social conditions*—that is, having to do with social mores and opinions and the relative climate they

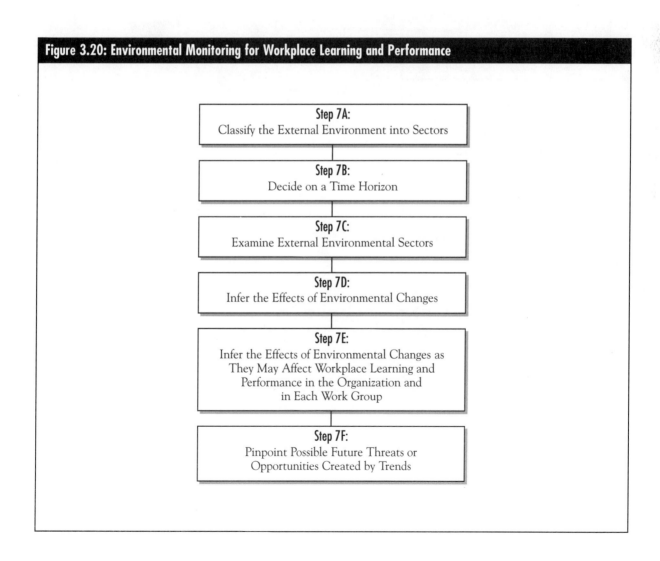

Figure 3.20: Environmental Monitoring for Workplace Learning and Performance

Step 7A:
Classify the External Environment into Sectors

Step 7B:
Decide on a Time Horizon

Step 7C:
Examine External Environmental Sectors

Step 7D:
Infer the Effects of Environmental Changes

Step 7E:
Infer the Effects of Environmental Changes as They May Affect Workplace Learning and Performance in the Organization and in Each Work Group

Step 7F:
Pinpoint Possible Future Threats or Opportunities Created by Trends

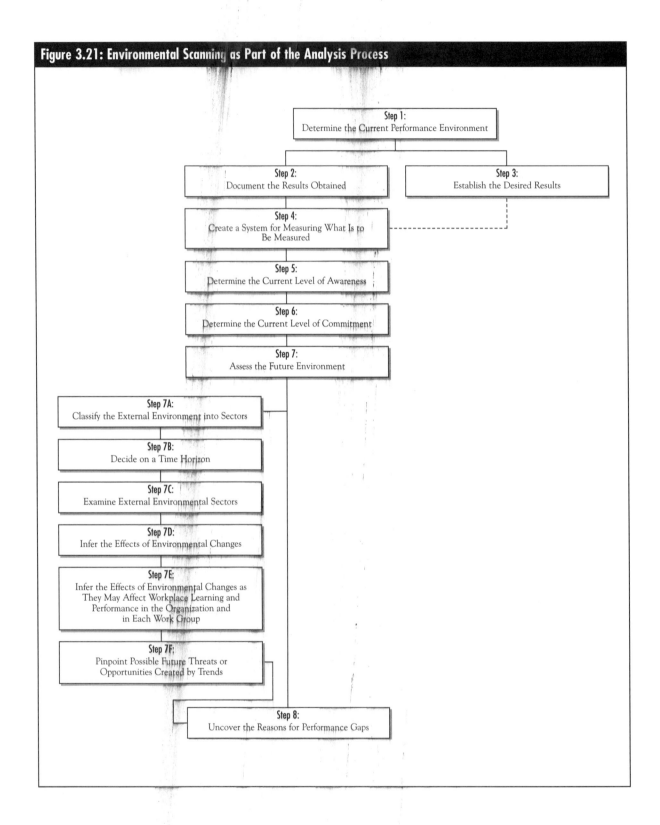

Step 1:
Determine the Current Performance Environment

Step 2:
Document the Results Obtained

Step 3:
Establish the Desired Results

Step 4:
Create a System for Measuring What Is to Be Measured

Step 5:
Determine the Current Level of Awareness

Step 6:
Determine the Current Level of Commitment

Step 7:
Assess the Future Environment

Step 7A:
Classify the External Environment into Sectors

Step 7B:
Decide on a Time Horizon

Step 7C:
Examine External Environmental Sectors

Step 7D:
Infer the Effects of Environmental Changes

Step 7E:
Infer the Effects of Environmental Changes as They May Affect Workplace Learning and Performance in the Organization and in Each Work Group

Step 7F:
Pinpoint Possible Future Threats or Opportunities Created by Trends

Step 8:
Uncover the Reasons for Performance Gaps

create for the organization in a nation, region, or globally

♦ *Market conditions*—that is, having to do with the business market and the relative climate it creates for the organization in a nation, region, or globally

♦ *Competitors inside the industry*—that is, those already doing business in the industry

♦ *Competitors outside the industry*—that is, those that are not yet doing business in the industry but are capable of either entering the industry or developing replacement technologies

♦ *Suppliers*—that is, individuals or other entities that supply the organization with its raw materials and necessary provisions

♦ *Distributors*—that is, individuals or organizations that distribute or transport the organization's product or otherwise help the organization reach its targeted customers

♦ *Geographic conditions*—that is, having to do with the location of key materials, suppliers, distributors, or customers

♦ *Technological conditions*—that is, having to do with tools, equipment, and work processes.

These sectors are depicted in figure 3.22.

Another way of classifying aspects of the environment, for purposes of examining the changes that would be expected to affect performance over time, would be to focus on trends that have been

Figure 3.22: Environmental Sectors

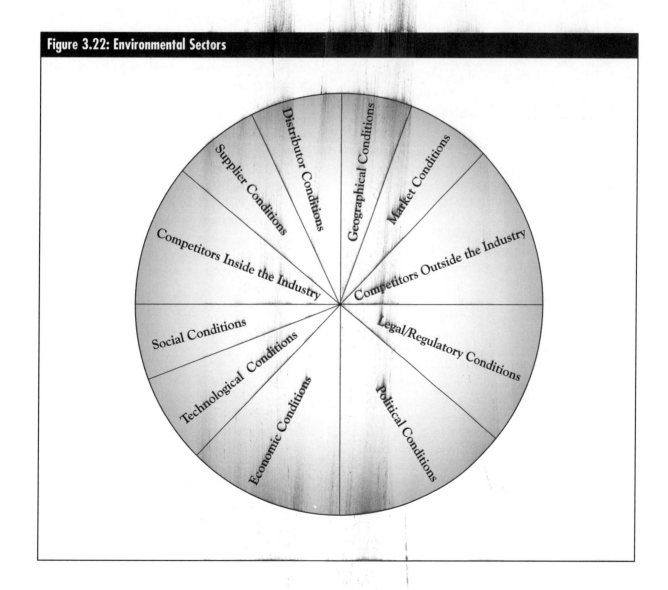

shown to be most likely to exert an influence over the workforce and workplace of the future (Rothwell, Prescott, and Taylor, 1998). For a given problem, the analyst may pose the following questions:

♦ What trends outside the organization might affect the problem most, and in what ways might those trends affect the shape of the problem in the future?

♦ If no action is taken on the problem now, how might changing technology influence the problem in the future? In what ways is the problem likely to be influenced by technological changes over time?

♦ If no action is taken on the problem now, how might changes in global economic conditions influence the problem in the future?

♦ If no action is taken on the problem now, how might the organization's continuing efforts to contain costs (through downsizing or other strategies) likely influence the problem in the future? In what ways is the problem likely to be influenced by the organization's continuing cost-containment efforts?

♦ If no action is taken on the problem now, how might the increasing speed of market change (that is, ever more rapidly changing consumer preferences) likely influence the problem in the future?

You can use the Step 7 section in figure 4.1 to organize your thinking about the influence of such trends on specific problems.

Step 7B requires that the analyst decide how long the scanning effort should take. The longer the time span for the prediction, the less likely that the prediction will be accurate. For example, 10 years ago it would have been hard to predict the pervasiveness of the Internet today. Similarly, it can be difficult to make accurate predictions about the impact of a potential performance problem, or even an existing one, far into the future.

Step 7C requires that the analyst examine external environmental sectors for expected changes, or impact, over the time horizon chosen. To do so, the analyst will need to talk to decision makers in the organization and perhaps to external consultants who are familiar with the industry. Step 7C is a kind

of forecasting that may depend on information that is subject to change at the time a decision must be made. Generating likely future scenarios is inherently a creative and abstract process.

Step 7D is a matter of inferring the effects of environmental changes on the general public; external stakeholders of the organization (anyone affected by a change or by a performance improvement intervention, and may include stockholders, public constituents, customers, suppliers, distributors, managers, and employees); departments or work groups in the organization; individuals in the organization; and job or work requirements. Step 7D makes Step 7C more specific, drawing conclusions about the likeliest futures for specific stakeholder groups.

Step 7E predicts the effects of environmental changes as they may affect WLP. In other words, how might trends and their impact on key stakeholders influence future learning needs? What will performers in the organization need to know and do to meet or exceed the needs of customers or other stakeholders? In other words, what learning needs—and what performance improvements—might be required in time to anticipate and thus avert organizational problems in the future?

Step 7F entails identifying the possible threats or opportunities that the trends create, and then mounting performance improvement interventions (or a comprehensive strategy for performance improvement consisting of numerous interventions) intended to avert future threats or seize future opportunities. Of the two possibilities, building a comprehensive strategy is preferable.

Vignette: As analyst, Ronetta Brown focuses her attention on what issues might affect turnover in the near future, including projected local and national employment conditions, the stage of the business cycle, the relative labor demand and supply, and other factors that are likely to change over the short term. To do so, she consults reports on the future demand and supply of labor in the industry and locale. In addition, she might read or talk to other business leaders in the area about projected labor demand and supply and about the wage rates of other local employers. She follows up these steps by asking the organization's decision makers questions such as these:

- What issues might affect turnover in the organization in the future? For instance, is it likely that the organization will be downsized, spun off, sold, or its ownership otherwise affected in a way that would make people worry about job security?

- What competitive issues in the industry might affect turnover? For instance, is it likely that a replacement technology will be invented or implemented that will dramatically affect the organization's need for personnel?

- What other issues might affect turnover in the future?

From the answers she receives, Brown can begin to draw some conclusions about the likelihood that shifting performance conditions will affect the performance problem with which the organization is attempting to cope.

Step 8: Uncover the Reasons for Performance Gaps

Definition and Purpose of Step 8

While previous steps have centered on *performance analysis*, or gathering information about performance and identifying or measuring gaps, *cause analysis* entails isolating the reason(s) for the problems. This is the second step in the HPI process model shown in figure 2.1, and it is also a role carried out by the analyst (see figure 3.23).

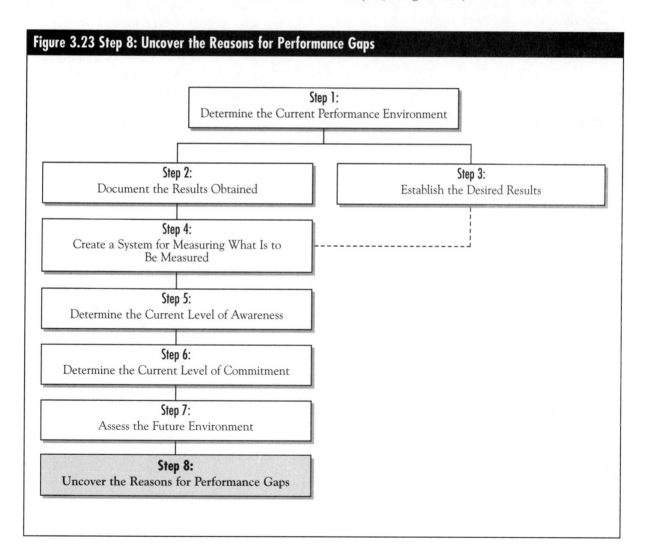

Figure 3.23 Step 8: Uncover the Reasons for Performance Gaps

Step 1:
Determine the Current Performance Environment

Step 2:
Document the Results Obtained

Step 3:
Establish the Desired Results

Step 4:
Create a System for Measuring What Is to Be Measured

Step 5:
Determine the Current Level of Awareness

Step 6:
Determine the Current Level of Commitment

Step 7:
Assess the Future Environment

Step 8:
Uncover the Reasons for Performance Gaps

Implementing Step 8

In 1988, Ferdinand Fournies, who wrote an important book about worker performance, isolated possible reasons for human performance problems. They may exist either in isolation or in combination. Performers

♦ do not know why they should perform in accordance with expectations

♦ do not know how to perform

♦ do not know what they are supposed to do to perform

♦ think their way of performing is better than the way you want them to perform

♦ think some other performance goal is more important than the one established

♦ experience no positive consequences from performing as desired

♦ think they are performing in accordance with what is desired

♦ are rewarded for not performing

♦ are punished for performing

♦ anticipate negative consequences from performing

♦ experience no negative consequences for poor performance

♦ face obstacles beyond their control that hinder, impede, or prevent them from performing effectively.

♦ face personal limits that prevent them from performing

♦ face personal problems that distract them from performing

♦ believe that nobody could perform as desired.

To identify or isolate these causes, pose the questions in the Step 8 section in the worksheet in figure 4.1 to people you think might be knowledgeable about the problem.

Each of the foregoing causes warrants elaboration.

When people do not know why they should perform, managers may have given them no reason to believe that achieving the desired results is worthwhile. Among other things, managers may not have clearly identified or communicated the organization's goals, or sufficiently dramatized them.

When people do not know how to perform, they may need instruction in what to do and how to do it through on-the-job, near-the-job, or off-the-job training. Alternatively, they might simply need practice in recalling how to perform an otherwise infrequently performed activity. Alternatively, they may need a job aid or some kind of performance support.

When people do not know what they are supposed to do to perform, it is likely they do not have a clear idea of what their job responsibilities, work activities, or desired results should be. Managers have either not made sufficiently clear what those expectations are, or not communicated them adequately, or both.

It could be also that performance standards have not been established in the first place. In that case, individuals have no way to self-assess performance, and managers have no way to hold them accountable for results. The upshot may be wide variations in performance.

When people think their way of performing is better than the way you want them to (in other words, if they have substituted their own performance goals for those defined by management or customers), they need compelling evidence why your goal is worth achieving.

When people think some other performance goal is more important than the one you have established, they will be inclined to devote time and effort to their own set of priorities.

Another way of saying what happens when people experience no positive consequences from performing as desired is that they have no "WIFM" ("what's in it for me?"). Too often the reward for working well is not money or recognition but more work (or more difficult work). These can act as disincentives; at the very least, they may fail to motivate people to perform in accordance with expectations. Conversely, the view expressed by some managers that "a paycheck is the only reward they should expect" can easily be felt to be patronizing, if not downright insulting. Such a view can thus be counterproductive.

When people are not performing in accordance with what is desired but think they are, it is probable that they are not receiving any feedback. They are *trying* to perform as desired—and, having heard nothing to the contrary, they assume they are.

One of the ways in which people can be said to be rewarded for not performing is when the organization has attached insufficient incentive to the performance desired. Another way is when the organization gives incentives for results other than those that are presumably desired. Naturally, people will pursue results for which they are rewarded.

When people are punished for performing, they are either being somehow penalized for achieving the desired goal or they are not receiving any benefit from achieving it. Among the former category, they may be subject to negative remarks by co-workers (who may, for example, accuse them of being management pawns, or of trying to stay on management's good side, or of being *ratebusters*—that is, people who exceed worker norms, such as informal limits on production that workers set among themselves).

Very much like the previous situation is when people *anticipate* negative consequences from performing. In this situation they believe that while they may not be directly punished for performing as desired, they will not benefit. For example, they might be reluctant to accept an assignment abroad for fear it could remove them from key decision makers at home, and thereby be damaging to long-term career prospects.

An example of what happens when people experience no negative consequences for poor performance is a production facility in which workers knowingly pass on defective products, confident that nothing untoward will happen to them if they do. Exacerbating this may be an environment in which they know they are being measured according to production, not quality.

Obstacles beyond people's control that hinder, impede, or prevent performance include those generated by management, such as failure to supply staff with necessary resources (time, money, personnel, equipment). In such cases workers often become embittered.

Personal limits that prevent people from performing include lack of ability, knowledge, or talent; for example, it makes no sense to ask someone who is illiterate to proofread. While this example may be extreme, it is not so unlike some promotion-from-within programs that use nothing more than seniority to evaluate candidates. The fault for failure lies not with the worker but with the organization that has established and maintained an ill-advised selection, transfer, or promotion policy. When the problem is systemic, the organization can correct the situation by altering its policies. When the problem is individual or isolated, it may require transfer or even

termination of the person who has been placed in a job that is over his or her head.

Personal problems that distract people from performing include crises in their lives off the job. Examples include divorce, custody battles, difficulties associated with childcare or eldercare, illnesses ranging from cancer to alcoholism, emotional difficulties such as depression—even speeding tickets.

If people believe that *nobody* could perform as desired, it is possible that management has established and communicated unreasonable expectations. To test a performance measure, a key question is whether anyone has ever performed at the prescribed level. Watch out if the answer is "No—and they never could, either, because it would be humanly impossible."

Research by this author (1996b) points to lack of feedback regarding work consequences as the single most common and significant cause of performance problems as perceived by WLP practitioners in the United States. Also playing major roles are lack of timely feedback on performance, lack of assigned responsibility, and lack of reward for performing as desired. According to the same study, the least common causes of performance problems in the United States are poor ergonomic design, lack of individual ability or talent, and lack of equipment.

There are many techniques that can be used to uncover the causes of performance problems. You will find several of them in Section 4 of this volume, including cause analysis, cause and effect diagrams, and process charting.

Vignette: To isolate the cause(s) of excess turnover XYZ Corporation, Ronetta Brown considers the many possible reasons that people are leaving. She interviews employees and managers; reads over exit interviews; studies recruitment, selection, and training methods; and watches how people interact with each other in performing work processes.

She weighs information that she has collected about criteria, perhaps comparing what (if anything) the organization does to control turnover to the "best practices" identified in the same or other industries. She also considers the causes of performance problems, listing in order the ones that are most likely affecting turnover. Finally she reports her findings to management and other stakeholders.

SECTION 1   GETTING STARTED

SECTION 2   DEFINING THE ROLE OF ANALYST

SECTION 3   ENACTING THE ROLE OF ANALYST

SECTION 4   TOOLS FOR CONDUCTING ANALYSIS

◆   Introduction to the Tools Section

SECTION 5   AFTERWORD

Introduction to the Tools Section

This section presents five tools:

1. **Worksheet to Guide Comprehensive Analysis:** From the time you think a performance problem exists, use figure 4.1 to guide you through the analytical process.

2. **Root Cause Analysis:** Use figure 4.2 to discover the underlying reasons for a performance problem. This approach is best used by assembling a group of workers who are knowledgeable about a problem and willing to ascertain its cause(s).

3. **Cause-and-Effect Diagram:** Figure 4.3 is another approach to discovering the possible reasons underlying a performance problem; it can be used instead of the root cause analysis technique. However, like root cause analysis, this diagram is best used with a group of workers who are knowledgeable about a problem and willing to ascertain its cause(s).

4. **Process Charting:** Use figure 4.4 to examine how work is conducted.

5. **Enclosed CD-ROM:** On the enclosed CD-ROM, you will find a comprehensive set of tools for conducting an analysis of your current level of analytical competencies, as well as a set of organizational analysis tools. The organizational analysis tools allow you to survey decision makers and other employees in your organization and determine if performance gaps are being caused by process issues, individual performer deficits, or organization alignment barriers. The competency assessment tools help you determine your current level of knowledge through two different means. You can take a post-test that is based on the content of the book. Your answers are automatically correlated to the analytical competencies. The program will create a road map for your future development based on your knowledge gaps. You also can administer a 360-degree survey instrument that will give you a well-rounded view of your current skill level. Gather the insights of your peers, your direct reports, and your supervisor to gain a deeper appreciation of your strengths and needs for development.

Figure 4.1: Worksheet to Guide Comprehensive Analysis

Directions: Use this tool to guide you from start to finish through a comprehensive analysis. You do not have to use every question, and you may wish to add more questions when appropriate. However, the idea of this tool is to give you a template to guide your questioning and analytical process.

Step 1: Determine the Current Performance Environment

1 How clearly do people understand the performance that is expected of them, and how much agreement exists that such performance is desirable?

2 How well can experienced performers recognize the situations in which they are expected to perform (that is, *identify performance cues*)?

3 How often do people receive feedback on their performance? How clear is the feedback they receive? In what forms do they receive it?

4 What tools, equipment, or other resources are essential to performance, and how many people have them when needed?

5 How often do people confront decisions or situations for which they believe greater authority is needed? How often is access to that authority actually necessary?

6 How organized are work processes? Will good, experienced performers agree on these processes? Can the processes be diagrammed?

7	In what ways are people provided with incentives for performing (before performance) and rewarded for performing (after performance)? Do they see what's in it for them?
8	How much do people value the rewards they receive and believe that the performance required to achieve those rewards is fair, possible to be achieved, and will result in the promised rewards?
9	Regarding new, possibly untried methods, how comfortable do performers feel about taking the risks to satisfy customers?
10	How are people trained? How is their knowledge kept current?
11	How are people recruited, selected, oriented, and advanced?
12	How does the allocation of human resources follow work requirements and production cycles?
13	How motivated are people to perform? How much do they want to achieve desired results?

(continued on next page)

Figure 4.1: Worksheet to Guide Comprehensive Analysis *(continued)*

Step 2: Document the Results Obtained

14	What is happening?

15	Who is involved?

16	How is the problem linked to the organization's business needs and/or strategic goals and objectives?

17	How much is the problem costing the organization, and how is it measured?

18	When did the problem first appear or become noticeable?

19	Where is the problem most evident? Are there geographical variations in the severity of the problem?

20	What steps have already been taken to solve the problem? What results have been obtained?

Step 3: Establish the Desired Results

21	What issues or trends in the work environment call for new action? Where are competitive conditions headed, and why?

22	What are the performance differences among the best-performing organizations in the industry, and how does the performance of these organizations (as judged by return on equity or other measures) compare to that of the organization in which you are conducting your analysis?

23	What are the differences between the highest-performing and the lowest-performing work units? Individuals? What accounts for those differences?

24	How should the organization provide guidance to performers about what is expected of them? How should disagreements be resolved?

25	What key business issues are affecting this organization? Which ones are most important, and why?

(continued on next page)

Step 3: Establish the Desired Results *(continued)*

26	How profitable is the organization at the present time? How profitable should it be in the future? What are the goals for profitability?
27	What are the return on investment (ROI) and return on equity (ROE) that the organization is currently realizing? What are the organization's goals for ROI and ROE? (If it is a large organization, which of its parts are realizing the greatest ROI and ROE, and why are those parts more successful than others?)
28	What is the organization's targeted market share? How was that target established? How realistic is it?
29	What are the targets for quality? What error rates have been targeted? How realistic are those targets? Have they ever been achieved?
30	What are the targets for customer satisfaction? How have they been identified, measured, and tracked? What feedback is given by whom about customer satisfaction to performers? How much should they be receiving?
31	What should be happening? What results or outcomes are desired?

32	Who should be involved to make that happen?
33	How will realization of the goal help meet the organization's business needs and/or achieve strategic goals and objectives?
34	When (over what time span) are the desired results to be achieved?
35	What are the interim goals, or milestones, that can be achieved toward realization of the ultimate goal?
36	What will the optimal state look like? What will be happening when it is achieved? What results will be obtained?
37	What steps have already been taken to create a vision or spell out the desired results? What level of agreement has been reached on them among decision makers?

Step 4: Create a System for Measuring What Is to Be Measured

38	What is the performance problem? *(Be as precise as possible in describing the gap between what results are presently being obtained and what results are desired.)*

(continued on next page)

(continued on next page)

Figure 4.1: Worksheet to Guide Comprehensive Analysis *(continued)*

Step 4: Create a System for Measuring What Is to Be Measured *(continued)*

39	How do people know that this is a problem? What tipped them off to this difference?
40	Describe how current results are *measured*. How do people know what results are being obtained now? Express the answer in terms of *quantity, quality, cost, time, customer service, or some combination of these.*
41	Describe what *measurable* results are desired. How will people recognize and measure the desired state when they see it?
42	What is the *economic value of current results*? Ask decision makers how much is being gained right now from current results.
43	What is the *economic value of desired results*? Ask decision makers how much would be gained if the desired results were achieved. What is that worth in nonfinancial terms?
44	What is the difference between the answers to questions 42 and 43 above? If present conditions were brought in line with desired conditions, how much money would be gained through additional revenues generated or costs saved?

45	How much agreement can you obtain for the figure(s) identified in response to question 44? Do decision makers generally agree that this sum represents the amount that "solving the problem" is worth? If not, why?

Step 5: Determine the Current Level of Awareness

46	How much are top managers in the organization aware of the problem?
47	How much are middle managers in the organization aware of the problem?
48	How much are supervisors in the organization aware of the problem?
49	How much are workers in the organization aware of the problem?
50	How much are top managers in the organization aware of the impact of the problem on the organization?
51	How much are middle managers in the organization aware of the impact of the problem on the organization?

(continued on next page)

Figure 4.1: Worksheet to Guide Comprehensive Analysis *(continued)*

Step 5: Determine the Current Level of Awareness *(continued)*

52	How much are supervisors in the organization aware of the impact of the problem on the organization?
53	How much are workers in the organization aware of the impact of the problem on the organization?

Step 6: Determine the Current Level of Commitment

54	How much are top managers in the organization generally committed to taking action to solve the problem as indicated by what they say?
55	How much are middle managers in the organization generally committed to taking action to solve the problem as indicated by what they say?
56	How much are supervisors in the organization generally committed to taking action to solve the problem as indicated by what they say?
57	How much are workers in the organization generally committed to taking action to solve the problem as indicated by what they say?

58	How much are top managers in the organization committed to taking action to solve the problem as indicated by their unwillingness to devote time, money, or personal attention to the problem?
59	How much are middle managers in the organization committed to taking action to solve the problem as indicated by their unwillingness to devote time, money, or personal attention to the problem?
60	How much are supervisors in the organization committed to taking action to solve the problem as indicated by their unwillingness to devote time, money, or personal attention to the problem?
61	How much are workers in the organization committed to taking action to solve the problem as indicated by their unwillingness to devote time, money, or personal attention to the problem?

Step 7: Assess the Future Environment

62	How could the external environment be classified into sectors?
63	What time horizon should be used for the scanning effort?

(continued on next page)

Figure 4.1: Worksheet to Guide Comprehensive Analysis *(continued)*

Step 7: Assess the Future Environment *(continued)*

64	What is likely to happen in the external environment in each sector over the time horizon that was selected?
65	What effects can be inferred from environmental changes on (a) the general public; (b) external stakeholders; (c) departments or work groups in the organization; (d) individuals in the organization; and (e) job or work requirements?
66	What effects can be inferred from environmental changes as they may affect workplace learning and performance in the organization and in each group?
67	What possible future threats or opportunities can be pinpointed by the trends?
68	What trends outside the organization might affect the problem most, and in what ways might those trends affect the shape of the problem in the future?
69	If no action is taken on the problem now, how might changing technology influence the problem in the future? In what ways will the problem likely be influenced by technological changes over time?

70	If no action is taken on the problem now, how might changes in global economic conditions influence the problem in the future?

71	If no action is taken on the problem now, how might the organization's continuing efforts to contain costs (through downsizing or other strategies) likely influence the problem in the future? In what ways will the problem likely be influenced by the organization's continuing cost-containment efforts?

72	If no action is taken on the problem now, how might the increasing speed in market change (that is, ever more rapidly changing consumer preferences) likely influence the problem in the future?

Step 8: Uncover the Reasons for Performance Gaps

The Problem (*describe it*):

How much of the problem is (or may be) attributable to the fact that performers:

73	do not know why they should perform in accordance with expectations.

74	do not know how to perform.

75	do not know what they are supposed to do to perform.

(continued on next page)

Step 8: Uncover the Reasons for Performance Gaps *(continued)*

76	think their way of performing is better than the way you want them to perform.
77	think some other performance goal is more important than the one established.
78	experience no positive consequences from performing as desired.
79	think they are performing in line with what is desired.
80	are rewarded for not performing.
81	are punished for performing.

82	anticipate negative consequences from performing.
83	experience no negative consequences for poor performance.
84	face obstacles beyond their control that hinder, impede, or prevent them from performing effectively.
85	face personal limits that prevent them from performing.
86	face personal problems that distract them from performing.
87	believe that nobody could perform as desired

Figure 4.2: Root Cause Analysis

Directions: Use this approach to uncover the causes of performance problems.

What Is Root Cause Analysis (RCA)?	RCA is an approach to getting at the reasons for a problem situation or event, helping to separate the presenting problem (the issue that has given rise to decision makers' concerns, or the consequences of a performance problem) from underlying causes.
When Is RCA Used?	Use RCA whenever a crisis event or situation occurs. Examples of such events or situations include: ♦ An accident ♦ A major mistake in production ♦ Loss of a major customer or client due to error ♦ A key decision maker complains about a problem.
Who Uses RCA?	RCA is part of the role of the analyst.
	Select a group of workers who are knowledgeable about the performance problem and ask them to
How Is RCA Carried Out?	1 list or describe the event(s) that occurred.
	2 identify the event(s) in which the performance problem has been most evident.
	3 determine the scope of the analysis.
	4 review the sequence of events for issues or causes leading up to the event.
	5 show relationships among contributing causes.
	6 assess the cause(s).
What Is Obtained from RCA?	The results of RCA should be depicted as a diagram of events, issues, or underlying causes leading up to the problem.

Where Can I Go for More Information About RCA?

Source: Wilson, Dell, and Anderson. *Root Cause Analysis: A Tool for Total Quality Management.* Milwaukee, WI: ASQC Quality Press, 1993.

Sample RCA Chart

Directions

Construct the chart using *Post-it Notes*,™ index cards, or sheets of paper on a wall

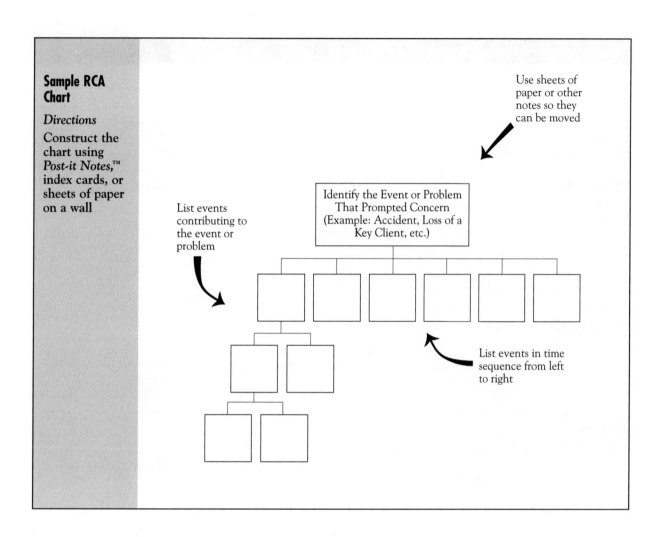

Use sheets of paper or other notes so they can be moved

List events contributing to the event or problem

Identify the Event or Problem That Prompted Concern (Example: Accident, Loss of a Key Client, etc.)

List events in time sequence from left to right

Figure 4.3: Cause-and-Effect Diagram

Note: A cause-and-effect diagram is also sometimes called an Ishikawa diagram or a fishbone diagram.

What Is a Cause-and-Effect Diagram (CED)?	A CED is a visual approach to identifying the component or contributing causes and effects of a problem.
When Is a Cause-and-Effect Diagram Used?	Use a CED to illustrate the elements of a work process or activity. Examples include: ♦ Steps in hiring a worker ♦ Steps in the manufacturing flow ♦ Steps in billing ♦ Steps in complaint handling
Who Uses CED?	CED is among the roles of the analyst.
	Select a group of workers who are knowledgeable about the performance problem and ask them to

How Is CED Done?	1	describe the problem.
	2	examine the relationship to the problem of each of several issues or elements. Ask the group to consider whether the causes of the performance problem stem from people, company policies and procedures, materials, tools and equipment, or other factors.
	3	list on the diagram the contributing factors to the problem.
	4	Consider how much each factor either helps cause the problem or is affected by the problem.

What Results Are Obtained From CED?	The CED should depict the contributing factors of a problem.

Where Can I Go for More Information About CED?

Source: Wilson, Dell, and Anderson. *Root Cause Analysis: A Tool for Total Quality Management.* Milwaukee, WI: ASQC Quality Press, 1993.

Sample CED

(Ask workers to enter names of people, policies or procedures, tools or equipment, or other factors contributing to the cause of the performance problem)

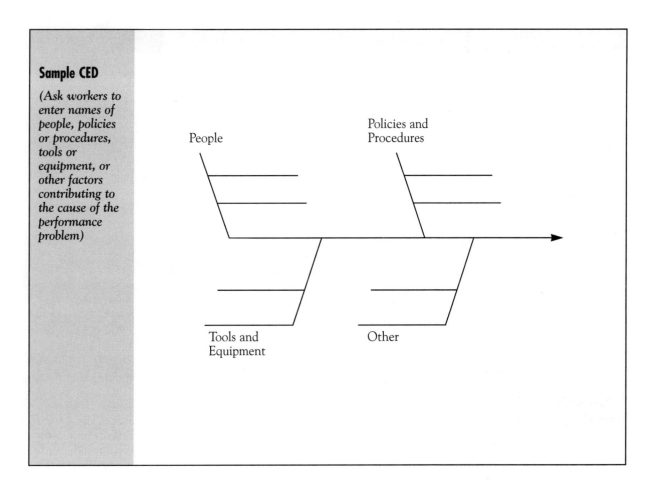

Figure 4.4: Process Charting

Definition: A process chart is a visual representation of a work process. It documents the steps that are taken when producing a product or service. Process charts help to uncover the barriers to a streamlined production process. The process chart works best when you suspect that the work is being done in an inefficient manner.

Directions: Select a group of workers who are knowledgeable about the performance problem and ask them to do the following:

How Is Process Charting Carried Out?	1	identify a work process.
	2	identify generally who does what in the process, and when.
	3	list the workers by exact name and title, what they do, and the sequence in which they do it. (This activity lends itself to small-group discussion.)
	4	review the current sequence of work that is conducted and determine where perceived or actual bottlenecks and duplications of effort are occurring.
What Results Are Obtained From a Process Chart?		Clarification of what happens in a work process, when it happens, and how to make the process more efficient.

Where Can I Go for More Information About Process Charts?

Source: Whiteley. *The Customer Driven Company: Moving From Talk to Action.* Reading, MA: Addison-Wesley, 1991.

Data Collection Tool

Directions: List individuals, job titles, and work groups in the far left column; list what those people do in the center column; and list the sequence in which they do it in the far right column; then look for any duplication of effort.

Individuals, Job Titles, or Work Groups	Tasks	Sequence of Work Flow Steps

SECTION 1	GETTING STARTED
SECTION 2	DEFINING THE ROLE OF ANALYST
SECTION 3	ENACTING THE ROLE OF ANALYST
SECTION 4	TOOLS FOR CONDUCTING ANALYSIS

| **SECTION 5** | **AFTERWORD** |

- ◆ Why Is It Important to Master the Role of Analyst and the Competencies Associated With It?

- ◆ How Does It Feel to Perform the Role of Analyst?

- ◆ What Should You Do Next?

SECTION 5   AFTERWORD

This section addresses three key issues:

1. Why is it important to master the role of analyst and the competencies associated with it?

2. How does it feel to perform the role of analyst?

3. What should you do next?

Why Is It Important to Master the Role of Analyst and the Competencies Associated With It?

Analysis is the WLP practitioner's first and most important role; without it, he or she cannot pinpoint the causes of a performance problem. In turn, a practitioner who cannot pinpoint a problem's causes will not be in a position to select, implement, or evaluate performance improvement interventions.

Since performance problems can have a multitude of possible causes, you may find that trying to isolate just a few of them is a significant challenge. But unless you are willing to settle for applying a single solution (for example, training) to all problems across-the-board, it is a challenge that you must meet.

The key lies partly in your attitude toward discovering and solving problems. To believe that in every case you will be able to determine conclusively the exact causes of a problem would be a mistake. Rather, your goal should be simply to present *clear evidence* that the actions and events that you have identified have a *high probability* of causing the given problem.

The danger of the first approach is that you will appear to be expressing a confidence in your recommendations that may very well exceed your ability to defend them; you then run the risk not just of seeming arrogant but also of damaging your credibility.

With the latter approach, by contrast, you will simply be setting forth the logical connection be-

tween the data you have gathered and the conclusions you have drawn. You're not suggesting that the data you've collected deal with every conceivable variable.

How Does It Feel to Perform the Role of Analyst?

Performing the role of analyst can feel a little bit like playing detective. Like good detectives, competent analysts remain objective and tenaciously seek out "just the facts, ma'am." Often the people who come to the analyst purportedly to seek help (line managers, for example) already feel they have found the source of a problem and selected the appropriate solution. They are impatient for action and are essentially looking to you not for analysis but for confirmation and implementation. To be effective, the WLP analyst must not be either intimidated or diverted; he or she must stick to collecting facts and reaching logical and independent conclusions.

What Should You Do Next?

As mentioned at the beginning of this volume, *The Analyst* is the first of several self-study job aids introduced in *ASTD Models for Workplace Learning and Performance* (1999). Subsequent volumes will focus on the other possible roles for the WLP practitioner: manager, intervention selector, intervention designer and developer, intervention implementor, change leader, and evaluator. Use them all to help build your competencies.

You might find it useful as well to refer to the CD-ROM that accompanies this volume and the volume on the evaluator's role. It can help you assess what you have learned from the text, assess your competencies, and identify actions you can take to help build those competencies.

BIBLIOGRAPHY

Alexander, G., and Lawrence, R. (1996). Creating a process improvement. *Journal for Quality and Participation,* 18–24.

Andrews, D., and Stalick, S. (1994). *Business reengineering: The survival guide.* Englewood Cliffs, NJ: Prentice-Hall.

Arnold, J. (1992). *The complete problem solver: A total system for competitive decision making.* New York: John Wiley & Sons.

Barrett, F. (1995). Creating appreciative learning cultures. *Organizational Dynamics, 24*(2), 36–49.

Benjamin, S. (1989). A closer look at needs analysis and needs assessment: Whatever happened to the systems approach? *Performance and Instruction, 28*(9), 12–16.

Biech, E. (1991). Diagnostic tools for total quality. *Info-line.* No. 9109. Alexandria, VA: ASTD.

Benson, T. (1992). IQS defines the gold. *Industry Week, 241*(2), 28–30.

Callahan, M. (1997). From training to performance consulting. *Info-line.* No. 9702. Alexandra, VA: ASTD.

Callahan, M. (Ed.). (1985). Be a better needs analyst. *Info-line.* No. 8502. Alexandria, VA: ASTD.

Cannie, J. (1994). *Turning lost customers into gold . . . and the art of achieving zero defections.* New York: AMACOM.

Chang, R. (1992). Continuous process improvement. *Info-line.* No. 9210. Alexandria, VA: ASTD.

Cottrell, D. (1991). Performance analysis: Holding up the bottom line. *Technical and Skills Training, 2*(8), 16–21.

Crosby, P. (1996). *Quality is still free: Making quality certain in uncertain times.* New York: McGraw-Hill.

Crosby, P. (1989). *Quality without tears: The art of hassle-free management.* New York: New American Library.

Deming, W. (1986). *Out of the crisis.* Cambridge, MA: MIT Press.

Denis, J., and Austin, B. (1992). A BASE(ic) course on job analysis. *Training & Development, 46*(7), 67–70.

Eisenhardt, K. (1992). Speed and strategic choice: Accelerating decision-making. *Planning Review, 20*(5), 30–32.

Elliott, P. (1996). Power-charging people's performance. *Training & Development, 50*(12), 46–49.

Fargher, J., Jr. (1992). Managing process improvement. *National Productivity Review, 11*(4), 533–547.

Fink, A. (Ed.). (1995). *The survey kit* (9 volumes). Thousand Oaks, CA: Sage.

Fisher, K. (1995). *Tips for teams: A ready reference for solving common team problems.* New York: McGraw-Hill.

Ford, J. (1993). Effects of organizational, training system, and individual characteristics on training director scanning practices. *Human Resource Development Quarterly, 4*(4), 333–351.

Fournies, F. (1988). *Why employees don't do what they're supposed to do, and what to do about it.* Blue Ridge Summit, PA: Tab Books.

Fox, W. (1987). *Effective group problem solving.* San Francisco: Jossey-Bass.

Gilbert, T. (1978, 1982). *Human competence: Engineering worthy performance.* New York: McGraw-Hill.

Gilley, J. (1992). Strategic planning for human resource development. *Info-line.* No. 9206. Alexandria, VA: ASTD.

Grant, J., and Gnyawali, D. (1996). Strategic process improvement through organizational learning. *Strategy and Leadership, 24*(3), 28–33.

Gretz, K., Drozdeck, S., and Lynn, G. (1992). *Empowering innovative people: How managers challenge, channel, and control the truly creative and talented.* Chicago: Probus Publishing.

Guy, M. (1986). Interdisciplinary conflict and organizational complexity. *Hospital and Health Services Administration, 31*(1), 111–121.

Hale, J., and Westgaard, O. (1995). *Achieving a leadership role for training.* New York: Quality Resources.

Hansen, G. (1994). *Automating business process reengineering: Breaking the TQM barrier.* Englewood Cliffs, NJ: Prentice-Hall.

Harless, J. (1997). *Analyzing human performance: Tools for achieving business results.* Alexandria, VA: ASTD.

Harless, J. (1989). Wasted behavior: A confession. *Training, 26*(5), 35–38.

Harless, J. (1975). *An ounce of analysis is worth a pound of objectives.* Newnan, GA: Harless Performance Guild.

Harless, J., and Elliott, P. (1991). Improving performance, achieving goals. *Technical and Skills Training, 2*(4), 8–12.

Hiebert, M., and Smallwood, W. (1987). Now for a completely different look at needs analysis. *Training and Development Journal, 41*(5), 75–79.

Hoffherr, G., Moran, J., and Nadler, G. (1994). *Breakthrough thinking in total quality management.* Englewood Cliffs, NJ: Prentice-Hall.

Holder, R. (1988). Enhancing intuition. *Quality Digest, 8*(2), 53–61.

Huse, P. (Ed.). (1998). *301 Great ideas for using technology.* Boston, MA: Inc. Publishing.

Johnson, S. and Flesher, J. (1993). Troubleshooting styles and training methods. *Technical and Skills Training, 4*(8), 15–19.

Jonassen, D. (1989). Performance analysis. *Performance and Instruction, 28*(4), 15–23.

Juran, J. (1995). *Managerial breakthrough: The classic book on improving management performance* (2nd edition). New York: McGraw-Hill.

Juran, J. (1989). *Juran on leadership for quality: An executive handbook.* New York: Free Press.

Kaufman, R., and Valentine, G. (1989). Relating needs assessment and needs analysis. *Performance and Instruction, 28*(10), 10–14.

King, S. (1998). A practitioner verification of the human performance improvement analyst competencies and outputs among members of the International Society for Performance Improvement. Unpublished doctoral dissertation. University Park: Pennsylvania State University.

Korotkin, A. (1992). A taxonomic approach to integrating job analysis with training front-end analysis. *Performance Improvement Quarterly, 5*(3), 26–34.

Langdon, D. (1991). Performance technology in three paradigms. *Performance and Instruction, 30*(7), 1–7.

Leeds, D. (1995). *Smart questions.* New York: Berkeley Publishing Group.

Levinson, H. (1972). *Organizational diagnosis.* Cambridge, MA: Harvard University Press.

McClelland, S. (1995). *Organizational needs assessments: Design, facilitation, and analysis.* Westport, CT: Quorum Books.

McDermott, R., Mikulak, R., and Beauregard, M. (1993). *Employee-driven quality: Releasing the creative spirit of your organization through suggestion systems.* White Plains, NY: Quality Resources.

McLagan, P. (1989). *Models for HRD practice* (4 volumes). Alexandria, VA: ASTD.

Machievelli, N. (1950). *The prince and the discourses.* New York: Random House.

Mager, R. (1992). *What every manager should know about training, or "I've got a training problem . . . and other odd ideas.* Belmont, CA: Lake Publishing.

Mager, R. (1972). *Goal analysis.* Belmont, CA: Pitman Learning.

Mager, R., and Pipe, P. (1984). *Analyzing performance problems.* Belmont, CA: Pitman Learning.

Paulk, M., Curtis, B., Chrissi, M., and Weber, C. *The capability maturity model for software* (Version 1.1). Pittsburgh: Software Engineering Institute, Carnegie Mellon University (http://ricis.cl.uh.edu/process_maturity/CMM/TR24/tr24_c2.html#C211).

Peery, Newman S., Jr., and Salem, M. (1993). Strategic management of emerging human resource issues. *Human Resource Development Quarterly, 4*(1), 81–95.

Perry, J. (1995). Align the front end first. *Performance and Instruction, 34*(4), 11–14.

Quinlivan-Hall, D., and Renner, P. (1994). *In search of solutions: Sixty ways to guide your problem solving* (revised edition). San Francisco: Jossey-Bass/Pfeiffer.

Ralston, F. (1995). *Hidden dynamics: How emotions affect business performance and how you can harness their power for positive results.* New York: AMACOM.

Risher, H., and Fay, C. (1995). *The performance imperative: Strategies for enhancing workforce effectiveness.* San Francisco: Jossey-Bass.

Rossett, A. (1998). *First things fast: A handbook for performance analysis.* San Francisco: Jossey-Bass/Pfeiffer.

Rossett, A. (1992). Analysis of human performance problems. In H. Stolovich and E. Keeps (Eds.), *Handbook of human performance technology: A comprehensive guide for analyzing and solving performance problems in organizations.* San Francisco: Jossey-Bass, 97–113.

Rossett, A. (1987). *Training needs assessment.* Englewood Cliffs, NJ: Educational Technology Publications.

Rothwell, W. (1996a). *ASTD models for human performance improvement: Roles, competencies, and outputs.* Alexandria, VA: ASTD.

Rothwell, W. (1996b). *Beyond training and development: State-of-the-art strategies for enhancing human performance.* New York: AMACOM.

Rothwell, W., and Dubois, D. (Eds.). (1998). *In Action: Improving performance in organizations.* Alexandria, VA: ASTD.

Rothwell, W., and Kazanas, H. (1998). *Mastering the instructional design process: A systematic approach* (2nd edition). San Francisco: Jossey-Bass.

Rothwell, W., and Kazanas, H. (1994). *Human resource development: A strategic approach* (revised edition). Amherst, MA: Human Resource Development Press.

Rothwell, W., and Kazanas, H. (1994). *Improving on-the-job training: How to establish and operate a comprehensive OJT program.* San Francisco: Jossey-Bass.

Rothwell, W., and Kazanas, H. (1993). Developing management employees to cope with the moving target effect. *Performance and Instruction, 32*(8), 1–5.

Rothwell, W., and Lindholm, J. (1999). Competency identification, modeling, and assessment in the USA. *International Journal of Training and Development, 3*(2), 90–105.

Rothwell, W., Prescott, R., and Taylor, M. (1998). *Strategic human resource leader.* Palo Alto, CA: Davies-Black.

Rothwell, W., Sanders, E., and Soper, J. (1999). *ASTD models for workplace learning and performance: roles, competencies, and outputs.* Alexandria, VA: ASTD.

Rummler, G. (1996). In search of the holy performance grail. *Training & Development, 50*(4), 26–32.

Rummler, G. (1991). Managing the white space. *Training, 28*(1), 55–70.

Schaffer, R. (1991). Demand better results—and get them. *Harvard Business Review, 69*(2), 142–149.

Schappe, R. (1990). Role of measurement techniques in organization change. *Organization Development Journal, 8*(3), 1–7.

Schneier, C., Guthrie, J., and Olian, J. (1988). A practical approach to conducting and using the training needs assessment. *Public Personnel Management, 17*(2), 191–205.

Schuler, R. (1989). Scanning the environment: Planning for human resource management and organizational change. *Human Resource Planning: HR, 12*(4), 257–276.

Sleezer, C. (1996). Using performance analysis for training in an organization implementing integrated manufacturing: A case study. *Performance Improvement Quarterly, 9*(2), 25–41.

Sleezer, C. (1993). Tried and true performance analysis. *Training & Development, 47*(11), 52–54.

Sleezer, C. (1992). Needs assessment: Perspectives from the literature. *Performance Improvement Quarterly*, 5(2), 34–46.

Sleezer, C. (1991). Developing and validating the performance analysis for training model. *Human Resource Development Quarterly, 2*(4), 355–372.

Sleezer, C. (1990). *The development and validation of a performance analysis for training model.* St. Paul, MN: University of Minnesota.

Stamp, D. (1995). *The invisible assembly line: Boosting white-collar productivity in the new economy.* New York: AMACOM.

Steps in human performance analysis. (1996). *Training & Development, 50*(12), 48, 1996.

Swanson, R. (1994). *Analysis for improving performance: Tools for diagnosing organizations and documenting workplace expertise.* San Francisco: Berrett-Koehler.

Swanson, R. (1988). *Forecasting financial benefits of human resource development.* San Francisco: Jossey-Bass.

Swanson, R., and Torraco, R. (1994). Technical training's challenges and goals. *Technical and Skills Training, 5*(7), 18–22.

Taylor, J., and Felten, D. (1993). *Performance by design: Sociotechnical systems in North America.* Englewood Cliffs, NJ: Prentice-Hall.

Tollison, P. (1988). Can participation improve a needs analysis? *Journal for Quality and Participation, 11*(4), 26–27.

Watkins, R., and Kaufman, R. (1996). An update on relating needs assessment and needs analysis. *Performance Improvement, 35*(10), 10–13.

Whiteley, R. (1991). *The customer-driven company: Moving from talk to action.* Reading, MA: Addison-Wesley.

Wilson, P., Dell, L., and Anderson, G. (1993). *Root case analysis: A tool for total quality management.* Milwaukee, WI: ASQC Quality Press.

Wright, V. (1993). There are case studies . . . and case studies. *Performance and Instruction, 32*(2), 31–33.

Wycoff, J. (1995). *Transformation thinking: Tools and techniques that open the door to powerful new thinking for every member of your organization.* New York: Berkeley Books.

◢ ABOUT THE AUTHOR

William J. Rothwell is professor of human resource development in the Department of Adult Education, Instructional Systems, and Workforce Education and Development in the College of Education on the University Park Campus of the Pennsylvania State University and director of Penn State's Institute for Research in Training and Development. He also is president of Rothwell and Associates, a private consulting firm with more than 30 multinational corporations on its client list.

Previously, Rothwell was assistant vice president and director of management development for the Franklin Life Insurance Company, Springfield, Illinois, and training director for the Illinois Office of Auditor General. He holds a Ph.D. from the University of Illinois at Urbana-Champaign and has worked full-time in human resource management and employee training and development since 1979, combining real-world experience with academic and consulting experience.

Rothwell's latest publications include *Building In-house Leadership and Management Development Programs* (with H. Kazanas, 2000); *The Competency Toolkit* (with D. Dubois, 2000); *ASTD Models for Workplace Learning and Performance* (with Ethan Sanders and Jeffrey Soper, 1999); *The Action Learning Guidebook* (with K. Sensenig, as editors, 1999); *Sourcebook for Self-Directed Learning* (as editor, 1999); *Creating, Measuring and Documenting Service Impact: A Capacity Building Resource: Rationales, Models, Activities, Methods, Techniques, Instruments* (1998); *In Action: Improving Human Performance* (with D. Dubois, as editors, 1998); *Strategic Human Resource Leader: How to Help Your Organization Manage the Six Trends Affecting the Workforce* (with Prescott and Taylor, as editors, 1998); *In Action: Linking HRD and Organizational Strategy* (as editor, 1998); and *Mastering the Instructional Design Process: A Systematic Approach* (with H. Kazanas, 2nd edition, 1998).

Letters can be addressed to the author at 305C Keller Building, University Park, PA 16803. He can be reached via email at wjr9@psu.edu.